Dedication

The James City Poets would like to dedicate this ... and mentor, Ed Lull.

He is a poet's poet. His knowledge of and adherence to style and form is impeccable. He holds us to those same high standards and we are all better poets because of him. Thank you, Ed, for all you have taught us and for all you have done to promote poetry in Virginia.

Ed is a Life Member of the Poetry Society of Virginia and served four terms as its president. In 2012, he was awarded the "Emyl Jenkins Award," for "inspiring writing and writing education in Virginia."

Captured Moments, an anthology (James City Poets)
© High Tide Publications, Inc., 2017

All rights reserved.

Individual copyrights are held by each author.
For a complete list, see the Table of Contents that follows.

All rights reserved. No part of this publication may be reproduced, transmitted in any form or by any means, electronic or mechanical, including photocopy, recording, or any information storage and retrieval system, without permission in writing from the publisher.

Names, characters, places, and incidents are either the product of the author's imagination or memory and are used as literary devices. In order to maintain subject anonymity in some instances, the authors may have changed the names of individuals and places or changed some identifying characteristics and details such as physical properties, occupations, and places of residence.

ISBN 978-1945990151
First Edition 2017

Book design: Firebelliedfrog.com
Edited by Edward Lull and Narielle Living

Published by:
  High Tide Publications, Inc.
  1000 Bland Point Road
  Deltaville, Virginia 23043

Find us on the World Wide Web at:
www.HighTidePublications.com

Printed in the United States of America

On the Cover
Hummingbird **by Peggy Newcomb**

Table of Contents

Dedication	1
On the Cover	2
Hummingbird by Peggy Newcomb	
About The James City Poets	3

The Poetry of Joan Ellen Casey — Sung and Unsung Heroes
When Irish Eyes Are Smiling	4
Losing A Loved One	5
And Becoming Oneself	5
Frogs	5
I Can't Imagine How, But the Spirit Goes On	6
Could It Be Other Than Ordinary Courage	7
This Is Not About Me	7

The Poetry of Gillian Dawson — Love, Cry, Laugh
Joy	8
Sonnet To Fresh-Baked Bread	8
From The Mountaintop	8
Rat Tale	8
The Homecoming	9
Story in Bronze	9
The Passing of Greatness	10
Techno-Love	10
Leaf Cycle	10
Your Poem	10
The Straight and Narrow Path	10
The Messengers	11
Villanelle to the D-Day Memorial	11
Near Bedford, Virginia	11
Elegy For Sergeant Reckless	11

The Poetry of Sharon Canfield Dorsey — Walk With Me
The Valentine Dance	12
Walk With Me	12
A Place Called Home	12
The "Run For the Wall"	13
Reboot	13
Love Is Strange	13
The Santa Safari	13
Happiness Sits Softly	14
Love Is A Perfect Pineapple	14
Zinnias For Don	14
Aftermath	14
Time, The Conqueror	14
The Savior Isn't Coming	15
Summer's Last Hurrah	15
Life In The Shadows	15

The Poetry of Linda Dunnigan — Ramblings
Mirrors, Reflections, Shoes, and Life	16
Rambling	16
All Things Old Must Sometimes Go	16
The Smile	16
The Memory Garden	17
The Arboreal Giant	17
The Woodland Dragon	17
Where Fairies Play	17
So Far Away, and Yet So Very Near	17
Simplicity and Tranquility	18
Christmas Pause and Ponder	18
Father Time and Mother Nature	18
Sights and Sounds of Fall	18
The Spider's Lair	18
Observation	18

The Poetry of Cynthia Frezek — Stardust

Atom Arrangement	19
Celestial Sky	19
Pay Attention!	19
Stardust	19
Passing of Time	20
Memorial For a Friend	20
Sacred Texts	20
I Can Imagine a New Nothing in the Universe	20
Mountain Dreams	21
Prophesy	21
Feathered Gatherings	21
Preserve Our Woods!	21
Falling	21
Still Out There	21

The Poetry of Edward W. Lull — And Life Goes On

My Oval Landscape	22
55 at Fifty	22
An Epiphany	23
Resolution	23
Ode To A Gnat	23
And Life Goes On	23
The Time For Change	24
A Lesson Learned	24
Coincidental Metaphor	24
A Squirrel's Lament	25
The Leader is …	25
The False Start	25
The Ballad of Deliverance	26
The Legacy	26
Mercury	26

The Poetry of Peggy Newcomb — Down Mountain Laurel Lane

Wedding Memories	27
Who Wants To Listen To the Clock?	27
My Trip To Wonderland	28
February 14th	28
Who Wrote This Play?	29
Checkpoint Charlie Museum, Berlin	29
The Back Porch	29
Gardens	29
Looking Forward Through a Rear View Mirror	30
The Reunion	30
Thoughts While Listening	31
To a Classical Concert	31
Yesteryear	31
What Is Christmas?	31

The Poetry of Adele Richards Oberbelman — Reflections

Decline	32
My Father's Garden	32
Time Limit (on Grief)	32
Live Long and Prosper	33
The First Moon Landing	33
Dream Catcher	33
Exotic, Erotic Artichokes	33
My Child	34
Consider the Crow	34
The Difference	34
Beautiful Mountain at Montebello	34
Chinese Puzzle	35
The Question	35
Wild Geese	35
Forgiveness and Grace	35

The Poetry of Linda Kennedy Partee — Windmills

Lost Abundance	36
Eden's Garden	36
Sea Life	36
Women of a Certain Age	37
Tangled Roots	37
The Family Tree	37
Salem Soliloquy	38
Pomp & Circumstances	38
The Taste Of Conversation	38
A Capitol Affair	39
Dancing The Seasons	39
Dancing Moonlight Garden	39
Heartsong	39
A Reckoning	40
Saint Augustine In His Cell	40

The Poetry of Mark Reardon — Roots and Wings

Roots and Wings	41
First Love	41
Spring Cleaning	41
I Fell In Love With You Anew	42
Lucinda	42
Mom	42
Sunday Morning Services	43
Neil	43
The Power of Children To Change One's Life	43
Dad	43
Pet Peeve	44
Kindness	44
Cody	44
Show Me	44
A Child's Love Will Overcome All	44

The Poetry of Terry Shephard — The Way We Love

Life's Moment	45
I Write	45
I Dreamed	45
Struck by Cupid's Arrow	45
What We Leave Behind	46
Vibrations of Voice	46
Butterfly Glide	47
Ode to My Lost Uterus	47
In His Wallet	47
Secret Love	47
The "Art of Aging"	48
Mortality	48
Flight	48
The Letting Go	48

About The James City Poets

In 2008, the poetry students attending the Beginning Poetry Writing Workshop of the Christopher Wren Association (at William & Mary) had established a social relationship as well as a desire to continue to improve their poetry-writing skills. The workshop leader, Ed Lull, a member of the Williamsburg Poetry Workshop at the time, decided to initiate a new workshop to accommodate the new poets; it was named the James City Poets (JCP) Workshop. The members agreed to meet twice a month from September to June, a practice that is still in place. In the ensuing nine years, some of the original members moved on and new ones joined to reach its current membership of eleven poets. In 2013, eight JCP members joined with nine members of the Williamsburg Poetry Workshop to produce an anthology entitled Distant Horizons. Now, in 2017, with the encouragement of our publisher, High Tide Publications, Inc. the James City Poets are proud to present their first solo anthology, Captured Moments. All eleven members contributed work to this volume, bringing their varied backgrounds, styles, and poetic voices for your enjoyment.

The Poetry of Joan Ellen Casey
Sung and Unsung Heroes

Joan's career went from editor for New York publishers to free-lance writer. Among her accomplishments: curriculum for the U.S. Office of Economic Opportunity, a teachers' and students' guide to Colonial Williamsburg, doctoral thesis on adults "making meaning," and a Metrorail Public Art Project Award from the Poetry Society of Virginia. Her real passion is poetry, where she has found a home for her diverse interests, painterly eye, and avid reader's palette. Her poetry has been published in various anthologies: "Distant Horizons," "The Poet's Domain" (volumes 29, 30, and 31), and in the Newsletter of the Poetry Society of Virginia.

When Irish Eyes Are Smiling

She called herself Marion Kate with a "K,"
though baptized Mary Catherine.
She had a shine in her eyes,
a blush of sherry on her cheeks,
and a long green scarf to make her look thinner.

In a brogue, broken only to twitter,
she talked of the butcher saving her fresh cuts of tripe,
the parish priest cuffing her hooligan sons, and
the doctor making house calls as if only for her.

With nails lacquered crimson,
hair coiffed, never gray,
adorned with costume jewelry,
she thought herself a grand lady
as if she never worked as a house maid.

Well into her eighties, she escorted
the "old folks" to play the ponies or ply slot machines,
and led them in song –
"When Irish eyes are smiling…"

There's a tear in your eye,
And I'm wondering why,
For it never should be there at all.

The day was soft they say in Sneem
when Marion was born.
Other births followed quickly of children who lived
and children who died,
until her mother was taken with the consumption.

Just ten, Marion mothered the brood as best she knew;
then the maid became the wife,
making the house too small, so
Marion was shipped to Australia,
to relatives she never knew.

There are no photos, or documents,
or any stories she told.
We can only imagine she walked
into a New York Schraft's one day looking for a job
with a small suitcase at age twenty-two.

Her prince, an older man,
arrived on horse – part of New York's mounted force.
Births of children followed quickly.
Some lived, some died
and she mothered the brood as best she knew.

…With such pow'r in your smile,
Sure a stone you'd beguile,
So there's never a teardrop should fall.

When golden years finally came
a pastel house was purchased in the "old country,"
but "the other side" was not what was remembered
except for clouds each day,
and then her husband passed away.

His death was followed by the death
of her grandchildren's parents, leaving
Marion wondering who lived, who died?
Still she heated the store-bought apple pies
and served them up as home-made.

For your smile is a part
Of the love in your heart,
And it makes even sunshine more bright.

After losing family, friends, and memories of them,
Marion sat with crumbs of soda bread in her lap.
"Oh, I've lived too long – I'm ready to go,"
she said sheepishly,
"but first let's have a big party."

And when Irish eyes are smiling,
Sure they steal your heart away.

Losing A Loved One And Becoming Oneself

For preventing an explosion that would kill many,
Ada's husband was wrongfully murdered.
Although he was exonerated, Ada left her dreams
and all she knew in Genoa and sailed to the states
with her young daughter, a few mementos,
and memories of love.

It was easy to imagine Ada in a fashion show
walking down the runway in a well-tailored outfit
that she transformed from a designer's sketch.
Her small frame held powerful presence,
her features, like chiseled Italian marble,
commanded a second look.

Ada's desire for quality of life and her skills
positioned her well in New York's fashion world.
She survived breast cancer and Hell's Kitchen
and spent resources on her child's schooling,
trips to Italy to keep relatives, customs, and
memories of her fallen husband alive.

Some people lose themselves in the loss of a loved one
but Ada was determined to take on life in her terms.
She loved again, a man she met on the boat to America
but refused to marry so as not to be another woman
in Angelo's house with Angelo's mother and sister.
After celebrating fifty years together, she buried him.

"Life was good until ninety," she said, "then I got old."
When the troubles of aging came, her world got smaller.
No amount of her will could determine more
than the black dye for her hair or the color blue she wore.
But she didn't let go for another seven years,
until she reached the twenty second day of the month,
a number Angelo always considered his luckiest.

Frogs

Susan glanced through the glass.
"You collect frogs?" she asked.
"No," I simply said
not to take too much time,
but she went on
"There must be dozens of frogs here
in silver, alabaster, marble, and wood
and is that one cloisonné?"
"Yes, and it's a box," I said
yielding to her gentle prod
to tell her about the frogs.

With my hand around the green and golden thing
I lifted its head to reveal
a long silver paper posing as a tongue
on which was printed one word – rivet.
She laughed as did I, now eager to tell her why
my house had become home
to a frog bowl and towel, apron and bookmark
where frogs hold keys, candles, and kisses
and decorate a kitchen with magnets, one of which reads:
If you eat a frog in the morning, nothing worse will happen
to you for the rest of the day.

The frogs have come mostly from one friend I said
but some have been given to me by those
who think I collect frogs.
You see, I haven't had the heart to tell anyone
when confronted by their glee
in bestowing on me yet another frog
that a frog was just for my giving
my appreciation to my friend
who took me and my children to a place
where we saw and heard so many frogs
and we sang and danced as if we were the Sound of Music.

It was there I awoke one night
thinking I too had just been buried with my mother,
but the croaking from the stream
reminded me of living and put my fears and grief to rest.
Then, at a country fair,
I found a small box with a frog inside to give her
for the beautiful memories she gave me.
Through the years of birthday and holiday giving
I delighted in finding her another frog, and so did she
for me. Soon others started gifting frogs.

I led Susan upstairs, past the shower curtain of frogs
and those nestled on a bed.
My husband and I are called the "frog people" I said
by my friend's grandchildren who say we started it all.
As we neared a frog on an Egyptian letter opener
sitting next to a French frog pen, I spoke with surprise
at the variety of frogs that are fashioned in poses
to capture the feats of so many myths.
I said pointing to a picture of my friend
embracing a large sculpted frog,
"but she's the one who started it all
and still believes there's a prince or princess in every toad."

I Can't Imagine How, But the Spirit Goes On

After months of waiting for a baby brother to play with,
he stole my crib and he stole my mom,
leaving me Bertrum and Natoss, my imaginary friends,
who stayed with me even after they took my brother away
because he stopped moving at age two
with polio they said.
I can't imagine how, but the spirit goes on.

So I went to school with the big kids
while mom took the bus far away to help him she said
because he could only move his pinkie by himself,
and say "good bye," as she left him there day after day
until he turned three
and could sort of walk with braces.
I can't imagine how, but the spirit goes on.

He had a lot of catching up to do about kids and playing,
not bringing alley cats home
or singing *Old MacDonald Had a Farm* in church.
Then he learned how to play dumb so I got blamed for stuff
he did. He also became the biggest tease,
even put water bugs in my bed.
I can't imagine how, but the spirit goes on.

Despite fights over the last piece of plum cake,
whose turn it was to walk the dog,
or the family TV always tuned to ball games,
we became friends. I even went fishing with him and
we hung out in New York bars looking for suitable mates,
giving comfort to our disappointments.
I can't imagine how, but the spirit goes on.

Through years of kid-growing – he had four boys,
I had three girls – he shaved his mustache,
I moved cross country, and we consoled one another
by phone about the perils of parenting.
There was little time to share much living
in those years too busy to even note their passing.
I can't imagine how, but the spirit goes on.

Our careers melded into one long day of building
resumes with paper degrees and achievements,
we sneered or cheered until it was time to retire
the war chest of stress and pay-down debt
that robbed our souls and left us on the dark side of moon –
save for a family gathering or two.
I can't imagine how, but the spirit goes on.

One day his skin started to shred, from head to toe,
layer after layer, until so weak and thin, it just broke.
An extremely rare genetic condition they said,
which could go away with a year of chemo
as long as he would stay out of the sun
and give up retirement plans to fish and garden.
I can't imagine how, but the spirit goes on.

Those were the days, my friend, we spent with
recordings of old songs to "listen to the words," you said.
So while I heard the *Piano Man* play me a memory
thinking of how you suffered for your sanity that year,
you imagined my lonely days of an empty dance card.
And we learned about each other
through words we could never say, listening to
Where Are the Clowns? There ought to be clowns.
I can't imagine how, but the spirit goes on.

As those days slipped by, you lost your footing
and carried a wooden stick "to chase away the bears,"
but your breathing grew difficult and your speech slurred
amidst mounting fears that ghostly remains of polio returned
to reclaim muscles freed from its grip long ago.
So I spent days learning what I didn't want to know.
I can't imagine how, but the spirit goes on.

In the annals of the arsenals of disease
I found angels – a nurse called Sister Kenny,
who fought the paralysis of polio with movement,
and I found you, my brother, developer of a vaccine
designed to spare children from multiple shots
and further insure their protection
from life-robbing pathogens.
I can't imagine how, but the spirit goes on.

As our journey of life raced to the finish line,
I realized how much more I wanted to know
about the person in my life longer than any other.
I wondered too, about the spirit
with which we are thrust so alive into a world to survive
where more loving brings more sorrow to each goodbye.
I can't imagine how, but the spirit goes on.

Once more trees budded and shed their leaves
as test results eliminated each disease
but the incurable.
Hope became finding a missing coin for your collection
until what was left was yesterday.
Today, your memory is visible under a veil of cloud.
I can't imagine how, but the spirit goes on.

Could It Be Other Than Ordinary Courage

Courage was the name she gave her award-winning sculpture. It portrayed a woman's head tilted so far back on a long and slender neck that her eyes faced upward. I could never look at it without thinking of the accident that dislodged three cervical discs in its maker. Yet the statue's delicate features and soft curls, baked hard into clay, were alive with her beauty and strength.

The statue was created somewhere in the middle of her fifteen-year journey with pain. Surgery was offered, withdrawn, then performed; prescriptions for therapeutic shots, manipulations, exercises, and acupuncture were written and revised; while pain killers moved her through time dreaming of one day having a child – to love she said.

As her time of fruition dwindled with no more remedies in sight, she and her husband decided she would quit her job and prepare her body to conceive. She relinquished all pain killers harmful to a fetus, ate and moved in harmony with nature, and prepped herself on child rearing. There were days of discomfort that brought her to tears. She coped by cradling her swollen abdomen and singing to the infant that grew in her womb.

When her baby girl was born she named her with an ancient word for earth. She described the experience of holding her for the first time as love more intense than she could ever imagine. Within a short time, the child was diagnosed with acute acid reflux that wrecked her small frame with vomiting, gas, and pain. Laying her on her back increased the symptoms. So the mother held her upright. The mother's condition grew worse from sleepless nights and constant holding, but the mother knew pain and could not stop trying to sooth her child.

The child grew to smile at her mother and followed her into imaginary trips with birdsong, calypso dances, coos, ahs, and tickles. She even learned to wrinkle her nose to tell her mother the pain was coming. Could it be other than ordinary courage – the child learned from her mother?

This Is Not About Me

I called her Ann even at our first meeting
because she was so approachable.
She talked eagerly about the department
she set up when hired by Chrysler himself
to interpret a world-class art collection
in a Norfolk, Virginia museum.

Ann glided through the galleries,
like an exhibit of flowing skirt and artsy jewelry.
With a tinge of a British accent,
she spoke passionately about the passion of Rodin,
and created a "mental soother," like Matisse
all while exuding elegance and ease.

I left that day with infectious enthusiasm
to research her educational programs that
lead children through the kingdoms of Egypt.
Their excitement taught me what Ann wanted to teach –
"Museums bring mummies to life."

Through thirty years or so,
we shared stories of our girls –
she raised four on her own –
along with parties, friends, recipes, dreams,
and Christmas cards we designed.
Her drawings always joyful whimsy.

I have only attended some of the events
where Ann juried an art show or
was honored for community service
or contributions to her profession;
She danced delicately through praise
but was a fierce advocate for people and the arts.

Looking both more frail and more alive,
I sat by her as she walked me through her years,
looking at pictures of those in her life I never knew
like Britain's King George VII, she was related to.
"I put this together for my children," she said,
"This is not about me."

I left her one day worried about her
weeding her garden alone; but she worried
about my comfort with her heart machine as she
calmly showed me wires that went through skin,
so proud of having "all it takes" to be a test case,
and saying – "this is not about me."

Wanting to write the story of Ann,
I checked the internet for clips.
It was there I learned she sat at the Woolworth's next to
Negroes the waitress refused to serve.
When asked if she wanted coffee, Ann simply said,
"There's somebody else here before me."

One day, on my way to see her, I learned
she had just died, from a friend who sent me
selfies they had taken the night before.
The pictures said it all: "This is not about me."
The joy on her face was a lasting image
for those she left.

The Poetry of Gillian Dawson
Love, Cry, Laugh

Gillian Dawson grew up in England, where she received a Masters degree in French and Spanish. She lived in Australia for five years before coming to America in 1965. She and her husband and children came to Virginia in 1975, and settled in Williamsburg in 1985. She began writing mostly humorous poetry for the enjoyment of her colleagues in Colonial Williamsburg, where she worked as a Historical Interpreter for fourteen years, moving to the Museums in 1988 as a Museum Monitor. She began attending the Poetry Society of Virginia Saturday Poetry Series readings and then joined their Sunday afternoon poetry workshops. She took the Christopher Wren Association Beginner and Intermediate Poetry Writing classes. She is a member of the Poetry Society of Virginia and the James City Poets workshop.

Joy

Joy is the happiness
that does not depend on what happens.
It wells up inside us
unasked and unexpected,
when life takes a sharp left turn,
yet for a moment we only see:
the morning bird singing in the tree,
cotton ball clouds sailing overhead
in a deep blue sky,
the bud about to become a flower,
lovers walking hand in hand,
children playing,
a sudden burst of glorious music
from a neighbor's open window,
flooding the air, capturing your heart,
or whatever lifts your spirits.
These will abide
no matter what happens.

Rat Tale

Why can't all we humans be more like the rat?
By nature, on seeing another rat trapped
he'll work without ceasing until he succeeds,
in opening the trap to set that rat free.

When offered some chocolate, his favorite food,
he acts as though he's just not in the mood,
a task more important is first on his mind,
he must free his friend now, and not after he's dined.

And then you'll behold, once his brother rat's free
a scene that would likely amaze you and me,
the chocolate shared equally, friendship confirming,
oh why can't we all be like those we call vermin?

Oh why can't we all be unselfish like that?
Who would have thought we could learn from a rat
that sharing and caring, respect for the least,
are the oil on the wheels that turn conflict to peace?

From The Mountaintop

Proudly he stood on the mountaintop
from where, he told them
he could see the Promised Land.
And faith imbued every word.

A land, he said,
where all would be treated equally,
where everyone would have a chance.
And hope imbued every word.

In this land people would be judged
not by the color of their skin
but by the content of their character.
And love imbued every word.

He would not lead them to that land
but they struggled on without him,
inspired by his dream,
while faith, hope and love imbued every step.

Sonnet To Fresh-Baked Bread

The curtains drawn, gone light of winter's day,
the kitchen bright, the family well fed,
all characters assembled for the play,
at last I'll try my hand at fresh-baked bread.

Yeast is the prima donna of the show,
both volatile and fragile, hating cold,
on to the stage salt, sugar, water go,
while flour is the hero, strong and bold.

Then comes the kneading process, press and turn,
as characters begin to play their parts
in forming dough, that rises light and firm,
and smell of baking bread then warms our hearts.

So now, with winter's sadness forced to flee,
come share a loaf of fresh-baked bread with me.

Story in Bronze

Kalat the sculptor, no more Saddam's slave,
three bronze heads of the tyrant he had made
portrayed the grieving soldier and the girl,
"If they could talk what would they say?" he thought.

"Poor soldier, did you lose your friend?" she asks,
"I see the boots, the helmet and the gun.
Did bombs or bullets take his life away,
or was it what they call an I.E.D.?"

"Little girl, he was my friend indeed,
we fought together since the start of war,
he saved my life by giving up his own,
he'll always be a hero in my mind.

I miss my wife, my family, my friends,
the son I've never seen, so dear to me,
I long for home, for peace, the end of war,
but I will stay until my mission's done."

"Dear soldier, while you're here you have a home,
my parents will receive you into ours.
Together we will drink three cups of tea,
and welcome you into my family."

An Iraqi sculptor, Kalat, was for years forced to make the many hundreds of bronze busts of Saddam Hussein that dotted Baghdad. When the tyrant fell Kalat melted three of those heads and created a statue as a memorial to the American soldiers and their fallen comrades.

The statue depicts a soldier kneeling before his fallen comrade's helmet, boots and gun, and standing beside him a little Iraqi girl, arm outstretched, her hand touching his shoulder, comforting him as he mourns. The statue is now in the memorial museum at Fort Hood.

The Homecoming

My teacher told this tale today:
A father had two sons,
the elder stayed to mind the flocks,
the younger one sought fun.

His patrimony soon was spent,
famine was all around,
his hunger overcame his pride,
he set forth homeward bound.

His father saw him from afar,
could scarce believe the sight
but rushing forth with outstretched arms,
embraced him with delight.

"My father, I have sinned," he said,
"but if you will forgive,
your faithful servant I will be,
so long as you shall live."

His father felt no anger but
rejoiced to see his son,
"We'll kill the fatted calf," he cried,
"and dance till night is done."

"For he who was deemed lost is found,
feared dead, yet has not died,
the son I thought to see no more
I welcome to my side."

The elder brother heard the joy
his rage could not contain,
he strode to where his father sat,
and there poured forth his pain.

"My father, why did you not kill
the fatted calf for me?
My work has multiplied your flocks,
I've served you faithfully."

"My son, all that I have is yours,
my love for you stands firm,
but from you brother's homecoming
a great truth you must learn."

"A father's love does not deny
the wrong that has been done,
does not condone, does not forget,
but must forgive……his son."

The Passing of Greatness

Rolihlahia your name,
meaning 'troublemaker'
or 'pulling the branch of a tree'
Xhosa your people,
Thembu your tribe,
your clan is Madiba.
Descendant of kings, yet poor,
herder of sheep and cattle,
barefoot, your only clothing
an ochre-red blanket,
your home a lowly rondaval,
yet happy and loved,
as you learned from your elders
about fairness and justice, compassion and humility.

1932

But you seized the day of opportunity
and attended school, studied, became educated.
Now in a wider world you saw with pain and anger
the suffering of your people
under the oppression, discrimination and humiliation
of the system we named 'apartheid' or 'apartness.'
You led the protesters,
suffered years of cruel imprisonment,
yet emerged free of bitterness or desire for revenge
as leader of all the people, oppressors and oppressed.

Today as we mourn your death
we know your story will be told
to those yet unborn: the story of a man
who fought for reconciliation, truth and justice and won.

Nelson Mandela.

Techno-Love

They met upon a summer's day
he said she stole his heart away.
Once introduced, they both agreed
to work in perfect harmony.

To please him she met all demands,
and gladly obeyed his commands.
When he was turned on she was too,
she always tried her best to do.

But one day he became so sick
they rushed him to the best clinic.
He had internal surgery,
but made a full recovery.

When he returned she welcomed him,
told him how lonely she had been,
no one to tell her what to do.
He said "I don't remember you."

A kindly neighbor diagnosed
"The two must be reintroduced"
Now their link is even smoother -
my printer and my lap computer!

Leaf Cycle

A leaf is such a common sight
we find no cause to sing
as millions clothe the trees in green
when Winter yields to Spring.

We give no thanks that leaves provide
life-giving air to breathe,
absorb the earth's impurities,
it's done so silently.

They shelter lovers as they kiss,
the children as they play,
old people sit beneath their shade
to gossip time away.

And then, as though some artist-god
had come, paintbrush in hand,
they turn red, orange, yellow, brown,
and fall, as nature planned.

And we should celebrate the leaf,
that dies, yet is not dead,
which lives to nourish future life,
as root, seed, bud are fed.

Your Poem

Could you write a poem? I'm sure that you could,
You may have to wait 'till you're in the right mood,
then put pencil to paper and just start to write,
'cause a poem can say anything that you like.

Some poems have rhythm and rhyme, and some won't,
some are long, some are short, some have verse, and some don't,
but whatever you choose, for you it's just right,
'cause a poem can be anything that you like.

You can tell about Mum and Dad, sisters and brothers,
favorite pets, or games played with others,
a food that you hate, or a ride on your bike,
'cause a poem can tell what you like or don't like.

It can tell of your feelings, your thoughts, or your dreams,
it's a small part of you, whatever it means,
there's a whole world out there about which you can write,
you can choose for your poem whatever you like.

The Straight and Narrow Path

Mostar, Bosnia, 2003.
The path up the mountain was straight and narrow.
It led to the cross
that stood stark and lonely
among the grey rocks.
"Yes" said the young woman, our guide,
"Sometimes we climb up to the cross
to celebrate a saint's feast day.
But you must be careful,
if you leave the path
you will step on the land mines."

The Messengers

A little girl was curious to know
more about a man called Jesus Christ.
Her father said "That man lived long ago,
his message was that we treat all with love.

One Sunday, when in church, she chanced to see
a crucifix displayed upon the wall,
"Who's that?" she asked, "It's Jesus," said her Dad.
"Why did they kill him? It makes me so sad."

"They feared his message, thought it would cause strife;
they nailed him to a cross and there he died."
Her father's answer gave her food for thought,
"How could they kill one who preached only love?'

One day she had a holiday from school,
her father took her to the library,
a picture of a handsome man hung there,
"Who's he?" she asked her Dad, "what did he do?"

"That's Martin Luther King," her Dad replied,
"He led the march to justice for all folks,
so blacks and whites could live lives without fear,
and all could share the blessings of our land.

He said that from the mountain top he saw
a land where all were treated equally,
where all were judged by character, not skin."
"Oh Daddy, did they kill him too?" she cried.

Villanelle to the D-Day Memorial Near Bedford, Virginia

To valiant hearts all honor be,
to you who stormed the beach that day,
you gave your all to keep us free.

In landing craft you crossed the sea,
keeping your secret fears at bay.
To valiant hearts all honor be.

You strode ashore with bravery,
though gunfire put you in harm's way.
You gave your all to keep us free.

This monument for all to see
we dedicate to that fierce day.
To valiant hearts all honor be.

'Neath noble arch statues' beauty,
your strength and agony portray.
You gave your all to keep us free.

Virginia's mountains long will see
that memories won't fade away.
To valiant hearts all honor be,
you gave your all to keep us free.

Elegy For Sergeant Reckless

Camp Pendleton, proud home of the Marines,
displays a statue of a fearless horse
whose sides hold ammunition strapped in place.
Who is this horse, why is that statue there?

"We named her Sergeant Reckless, our Marine,
born into freedom on Mongolia's plains,
her master sold her to us in Korea,
we little knew what treasure we had bought.

She soon became our heroine in war,
across the dangerous paddy fields she strode,
up mountain paths the ammunition brought,
the wounded carried down upon her back.

Herself twice wounded, yet she carried on,
to save her friends, herself she scorned to save,
and we in turn protected her from harm,
flak jackets sacrificed when fire grew fierce.

When resting in the camp she made us laugh,
her favorite foods were for a horse quite strange,
don't leave your scrambled egg or Hersheys out,
and always put a lid upon your beer!

Camp Pendleton was her retirement home,
two Purple Hearts and numerous medals won,
from war she turned to fertile motherhood,
three little Recklesses she duly bore.

Our Sergeant Reckless passed away last May,
her body laid to rest by loving hands,
full military honors spoke her worth,
she was the bravest horse I've ever known."

The story of 'the little horse that could', Sergeant Reckless, her Korean name Ah Chim Ha, (Flame-in-the-morning), who served with a rifle platoon of the 5th Marines in the Korean war, bringing ammunition to the front lines. She died in 1968 at Camp Pendleton; a statue was erected there in her honor.

The Poetry of Sharon Canfield Dorsey
Walk With Me

Sharon Dorsey has published poetry, fiction, non-fiction, and juvenile fiction in magazines, newspapers, journals, and anthologies, including McCalls, Christian Singles, the Colonial Williamsburg News, Mature Living, the Poet's Domain, and others. She was editor of Expats International and a columnist for Ashland Oil Newsletter. Dorsey is a Vice President of the Poetry Society of Virginia (PSV), and a member of Pen Women International, Chesapeake Bay Writers, and James City Poets; she has won writing awards from PSV, the CNU Writer's Conference, Gulf Coast Writer's Association, and others. She has published a book of poetry, *Tapestry,* a memoir, *Daughter of the Mountains,* and a children's book, *Herman, the Hermit Crab and the Mystery of the Big, Black, Shiny Thing.*

The Valentine Dance

One by one, sleek limos deliver precious cargo,
boys in tuxedos, awkwardly clutching corsage boxes,
giggling girls in rainbow-hued gowns,
flitting, like butterflies across the school lawn.

Inside the transformed gymnasium,
the excited, young teens take their places,
boys on one side, girls on the other,
waiting expectantly under flower canopies.

The high school band executes a drum roll.
The principal and vice-principal step forward,
each holding a red box, trimmed in paper doily hearts.
A name is drawn from each box and announced.

The named boy and girl meet in the center of the room.
The boy bows and presents his corsage gift.
The girl curtseys as he places the flowers on her wrist.
They wait nervously as others are matched and join them.

When each has a partner, the band swings into high gear.
Misty-eyed parents peer from the sidelines
as couples gyrate to their favorite tunes,
awkwardness forgotten in the joy of the moment.

Tonight, no one is left standing on the sidelines.
Tonight, there will be no tears.
For one night, their special needs children
are just teenagers, attending their first dance.

(Inspired by the dances for special needs teens, held around the country and sponsored by the Tim Tebow Foundation.)

A Place Called Home

Twinkling lights greet me as I crest the last hill,
heading down into the small town I used to call home.
It's Christmas Eve; stores are still welcoming customers.
People scurry along the narrow street
clutching packages and excited children.
Light snow glitters in the street lights.

Not much has changed in this small town
of Charmco, West Virginia,
since I left it, fifty years ago.
The names on the buildings are the same,
Mosries Dress Shop, Virgil's Barbershop.
The Honky Tonk's sign still promises food and fun.

The vacant lot on the corner is overgrown,
a faded sign the only reminder of the Ferris Wheel
that used to terrify small children.
The outskirts of town reflect the changes –
a new Kroger Store, a sprawling sub-division,
a strip mall with a giant Walmart.

My destination lies three miles east,
a small frame house at the end of a steep drive,
surrounded by fruit trees and evergreens.
The windows are dark, the rooms empty.
My mother and father are long gone,
along with glowing trees and welcoming hugs.

My brother and his family await my arrival--
three doors away-- a lifetime away from this silent house.
I sit for a few minutes, savoring the stillness,
allowing the memories to dance through,
awakening the soul of this place,
a place called home

Walk With Me

Walk with me through forests of morning
as dawn scatters a path of silver before us
and you tell me you love me for the first time.

Walk with me through forests of mid-day
where heat blazes, tempering us, testing us
and I tell you I will love you forever.

Walk with me through forests of evening...
holding my hand as the sun sets behind us,
taking me back to a time
when you were by my side.

The "Run For the Wall"

They descended on the small mountain town
of Rainelle, West Virginia,
like swarms of noisy mosquitoes –
five hundred strong,
motorcycles of every size and noise decibel,
bound for the Vietnam Memorial in Washington, D. C.

Piloted by veterans of Vietnam, Iraq, Afghanistan
and every skirmish in between,
they thundered down the mountain,
into streets lined with families,
unemployed miners, disabled in wheelchairs,
all applauding, cheering and waving American flags.

For many years, this small coal mining town
has welcomed the "Wall" vets who travel to
D. C. each year to remember their fallen comrades.
The citizens of Rainelle feed them,
house as many as they can, and honor their sacrifices.
On the mountainside behind them, wave 1100 flags,
representing the war casualties from the state.

An event that started years ago with a small welcome picnic,
has become an immense celebration of remembrance.
Vets of all ages, men and women,
look forward each May to this reunion
with their West Virginia friends.
This year, the mobile Vietnam Casualties Wall
draws silent visitors and tears.

The "Run for the Wall" assures that those Americans
who paid the ultimate price for our freedom
are remembered and revered.

Reboot

I wish the world were color-blind.
I wish the world were fair.
I wish the world spoke kinder words.
I wish the world would care.

It's time, I think, to stand for change.
It's time to march for good.
It's time to love our fellow man.
It's time to say, "We stood."

We stood for peace and freedom's truth.
We stood with all who care.
We stood against the ones who hate.
We stood with those who dare.

A time will come when love prevails,
A time when hope will win.
A time when good will banish hate.
A time when we're all kin.

Love Is Strange

The chickadee approaches the window cautiously,
flying back and forth, fluttering closer,
teasing, backing off, then CONTACT,
pecking the glass as he helicopters in midair.

For three days, again and again,
he zeros in, pecks at the bird in the glass,
retreats a few feet, assesses the situation,
then helicopters in one more time.

I admire his persistence but worry
he will dive-bomb the glass and hurt himself.
I close the blinds, trying unsuccessfully
to dull the reflection that keeps him coming back.

I'm sure the chickadee is male,
based on memories of my own experiences
with a pre-teen boy with a crush.
Subtlety was never his strong suit either.

He also relied on teasing, and running away,
persistently chasing me around the playground,
once stealing a peck on the cheek,
then hiding behind a tree to watch me blush.

They're not so different,
the chickadee and my first suitor.
They were saying the same thing.
See me. See ME.

The Santa Safari

They tumble out of my house the same way they tumbled in,
sippy cup and mugs in hand, mini I-pads under their arms,
giggles echoing in the quiet, frosty after-Christmas morning.

Adaline, the nine-year-old,
big-sisters the little ones into their car seats.
Emma, the bright-eyed, five-year-old middle child,
tucks her new Cabbage Patch baby into the seat belt.

Zachary, the all-boy, four-year-old force of nature,
waves a battered Tigor, his irresistible dimpled face
half hidden behind a pacifier that he fights to keep.

Daughter-in-law, Amy, and son, Steven, circle the van,
tightening seat belts, squeezing in last minute snack bags,
fastening those ever-present I-pads to the backs of seats.

They are like a well-oiled machine, packing every space,
carefully tucking newly-acquired Christmas presents
into their digitally-equipped Santa sleigh on wheels.

Their visit has been a whirlwind, getting reacquainted with
grandchildren who are suddenly taller, and squeezing in
quiet catch-up talks by the fire after kids are in bed.

As I watch the firelight play on Steven's much-loved face,
I lament the fact that they live out of daily-hugging distance.
Kudos to these parents who could have stayed home
by their own fire.

The kids wave as our 2016 Christmas visit comes to an end.
The Santa safari van moves on to the next grandparent visit.
Happiness is ... all of us together, for three precious days.

Happiness Sits Softly

Happiness is like a butterfly,
the more you chase it, the more it will elude you.
Turn your thoughts to other things.
It comes and sits softly on your shoulder.

At 10, happiness was tangible - a shiny, new bike,
till I saw my friend's bike had a pink basket and mine didn't.

At 20, happiness was a shiny, new husband,
till he became a soldier and went to Korea for a long year.

At 30, happiness was a shiny new dream house,
till dreams were shattered and the house was left behind.

At 40, happiness was children and family life,
till infidelity reared it's ugly head.

At 50, happiness reappeared, in the form of a new soul mate.
I nurtured it, hoping it wouldn't fly away.

At 60, happiness was a home together.
I thanked the universe every night.

At 70, happiness was replaced by her alter ego, pain.
Death marched into Happy Valley,
leaving behind fear and destruction.
I wondered if life's pieces could be glued back together.

Happiness crept back, after a time, not as shiny, still elusive,
a Meadow Lark's song at dusk,
a grandchild's laughter,
a peaceful heart.
Like the butterfly on a summer day,
happiness sits softly on my shoulder.

Love Is A Perfect Pineapple

A glance in my rear-view mirror
reveals an unfolding family tableau.
Feeling a little guilty but curious,
I sit transfixed, unobtrusive, watching.

Two people are lifting an elderly man into a wheelchair.
The woman covers his gaunt frame with a plaid blanket.
A young man adjusts a white mask over his nose and mouth.
I wonder...wife and son?

They trundle him into the grocery store.
I follow, my own list in hand.
We separate at the door,
but cross paths again later as I wait at the check-out.

The wheelchair shopper is carefully surveying pineapples.
He picks one up, turns it, sniffs it and puts it back.
Again, choose, scrutinize, sniff, reject.
For once, I'm glad my check out line is slow.

After four rejections, he nods his head,
places the chosen fruit into the basket.
I catch a glimpse of twinkling eyes
and know he is smiling behind the white mask.

Over his head, the woman and man exchange smiles.
I feel tears welling in the back of my throat.
Happiness today is the search for a perfect pineapple.
Love is allowing the adventure to happen.

Zinnias For Don

I planted zinnias for Don today,
in shades of pink and fuchsia and yellow,
in earth warmed by spring sun
and softened by April rains.

I planted zinnias today and marigolds,
in gold and Tuscan orange,
seeds to grow and remind us,
spring's rebirth follows winter's darkness.

I planted life today for all of us he left behind,
who will love and protect and nurture each other,
as we remember,
as we always remember.

Aftermath

The days tumble over each other
like scarlet maple leaves in October.

It's morning; it's evening.
Did I eat lunch? I can't remember.

Children come by; friends call.
I don't recall our conversations.

The noise in my head drowns out everything.
The lump in my throat is suffocating.

I sleep but do not rest.
I cry but am not comforted.

I awaken in gray light of dawn,
sheets rumpled, pillow damp.

I reach out but no fingers curl around mine.
I hate the pragmatic voice of truth that murmurs,
"He's gone."

Time, The Conqueror

He came to me in the depth of darkness,
Death, majestic in his billowing cape,
quieting my fears, "Do not worry.
I will not come here again for many nights."

Peace came on an autumn afternoon,
telling me my lost loved ones were safe
and watching over me,
their spirits always in my heart.

Hope rode in on a white horse,
trailing a rainbow on a stormy day,
and carrying a gilded list of gratitudes
that I had ignored or forgotten.

Love enveloped me on a sunny Sunday,
reminding me that she had always been there,
in a friend's hug, in a child's smile,
in a promise kept of a better day.

Happiness skittered in and out,
like a nervous chickadee, wanting sustenance
but fearing to trust the hand that offered it,
till Time, the Conqueror, brought the ultimate gift,
healing.

The Savior Isn't Coming

The room is filled; the mood is grim.

The men are bent, older than their years.
Coal dust lingers in their lungs.
Their women are aged too, from worry,
from struggles to feed families.

These coal miners learned today,
they may lose their health care,
so a tax credit can be given to the wealthy.

The man they believed to be savior,
emerged as a Robin Hood,
who steals from the poor and gives to the rich.

He promised a new day for the coal mines.
They believed because they had no other hope.
The emerging truth is devastating.

Their stories unfold as the reporter questions...
the single Mom with a handicapped child,
that child cared for through Medicaid...

the disabled miner, unable to work,
who feeds his family with his welfare check,
gets his heart medication from Medicaid...

the widow, too old to work but
not quite old enough for Medicare.
What will she do if Medicaid is eliminated?

Fear is a living thing in this room,
a thing that robs people of their dignity,
and sadly, sometimes their lives.

These loyal voters got the memo today.
The savior isn't coming.
The savior doesn't care.
Is anyone out there listening to truth tonight?

Or, are we all in denial – watching "The Bachelor."

Summer's Last Hurrah

Cotton candy clouds paint the azure sky.
Playful waves kiss the beach, then retreat,
leaving behind shell treasures.

Tiny sandpipers skitter along the water's edge,
helping themselves to unsuspecting sand fleas.

A light October breeze reminds me,
summer is winding down, a fleeting luxury.

The sun's warmth on my shoulders is medicinal,
temporarily curing all aches and pains.

A flock of geese, headed south, honk goodbyes
that echo in the silence of afternoon.

I soak in the sun, the solitude, the peace,
grateful for summer's last hurrah

Life In The Shadows

He was a homeless alcoholic
and a drug addict.
He had no one who cared about him.
He lived in the woods behind the shopping center.
He was forty seven and had been a hard worker
till construction jobs dried up.

He had a family once, a wife, children.
But his best friends – drugs and alcohol,
drove them away.
When the wages stopped coming in,
the landlord threw him out.
Friends abandoned him, as his family had earlier.

Most days, he stood with a sign by the highway,
begging food to carry back to the tent in the woods.
Sometimes there was enough money to buy dry socks
but only after he bought the cheap wine or drugs
that put him to sleep at night
and awakened him with angry cravings in the morning.

One cold night, the lights of a church drew him in,
The small sanctuary was warm,
the people kind, welcoming.
They gave him food, clean clothes,
arranged for housing and they fed his soul.
He cried when he saw his own shower and a bed.

He entered counseling and became a fixture
at every service in the small church.
He did chores for the members to pay back.
One day, he didn't appear at church or his room.
They found him in the woods where he had lived.
His old friends, drugs and alcohol had won.

His church family buried him and grieved his passing.
They vowed to commemorate his life
by doing more to help others like him.
Every day now, homeless in our community benefit
from the program established in his name.
One hopes, he knows he was loved and is not forgotten.

The Poetry of Linda Dunnigan
Ramblings

Lynda, mother, grandmother and retired educator, grew up in a small mountain railroad town at the headwaters of the James River. She began writing poetry at an early age, using word to paint pictures of life, family, love, loss, and the natural world. Her poetry, both humorous and serious, invites the reader to reflect and draw comparisons to their own life experiences.

Mirrors, Reflections, Shoes, and Life

Whose face is that in the mirror? That aged face, can't be me. Lines and shadows reflecting life's journey lack the beauty of Da Vinci's old souls.

Oh, to capture what the artist's eye sees, not the wrinkles on my face, or the shuffle in my walk,
but life's journey and the memories.

Life, it seems, resembles a pair of well-worn shoes, stretched, creased, scuffed, well-worn and comfortable, there are many miles left on the soles.

Now, this old soul stands before the mirror, gazing through cataract clouded eyes beneath creased, shaggy brows. I squint, frown, then look down at feet no longer clad in shiny new shoes, but in well-worn slippers.

Ambling forward on creaking joints, steadied by walker or cane. My gate is less steady and my forward motion slower. But much like soles on well-worn shoes, despite wear and tear, there are years left in this worn old soul.

For you see, mirrors fail to reflect what my mind's eye sees, the enthusiasm in my voice, the twinkle in my eyes, and memories of my journey that keep me forever young.

Rambling

Nothing replaces the beauty of nature at twilight.
I stroll under the soft glow of the streetlight's shadow in air pungent with the scent of freshly mown grass. The neighborhood herd stands silently in the shadows, waiting for me to pass before disappearing into the woods. Serenaded by a cacophony of honking geese, crickets and frogs, I slowly make my way down to the pond. There, watching shifting shadows on now still waters, as I gaze at the moon's reflection, I quiet my mind, putting the ripples of the day to rest.
Then turning, I slowly make my way home, grateful for a peaceful ending to the day.

All Things Old Must Sometimes Go

All things old must sometime go.
Too soon, they are forgotten.
Not so the patchwork quilt
that smells of mothballs and cedar.

Old and worn garment scraps,
discarded fabrics, salvaged and stitched together,
wrap me in a blanket of warmth and cherished memories,
recapturing the fabric of time.

All things old must sometime go.
Some, though gone, are not forgotten.

The Smile

The warmth of the smile
on the face of a child
brightens the darkest of days.

And the joy in child's play
on a bright sunny day,
quickly chases
all worries away.

How I long to bring back those childhood years,
 chase away my doubts, dry all my tears,
 feel childhood's warmth and joy once again.

For over time, you see, joy has abated.
Life's troubles, it seems, have left me quite jaded.

I long to return to that happier time.
Oh, I long, once again, for warmth on my face.
For childhood innocence and joy to replace
my mind filled with sadness, with doubt and with fear.

Oh, to turn back time, and return for a while,
 to that happier time, the joy of that smile,
 and be free of troubled and worrisome days.

The Memory Garden

Today is an avalanche of yesterdays,
burying me in memories of a lifetime.

High atop the mountain
the wind blows.
Sheltered beneath the ageless holly,
I am buffeted by the wind,
yet warmed by a blanket of memories.
There, in the autumn of my life
I stand alone and mourn his loss.
For grief is the cost
of the love that was lost,

Then I stop and remember
that love never dies.
So though I now cry,
I don't question why,
instead, simply mourn his passing.
I'm not really alone
although he is gone,
for you see,
love is everlasting.

As I stand on the knoll, once again,
remembering my love and my friend,
watching life flashing by
in the blink of an eye,
I give thanks for the years that we shared.
Love, never lost, always present,
regardless of where we abide,
in my heart he will always be with me,
though no longer close, by my side.

The Arboreal Giant

I am uncertain how long it stood, weathering the elements.
Here long before house and yard replaced field and woods,
its majestic canopy providing shade and shelter.

Once, tasty hickory nuts fell from its branches.
Now, its leafless branches crash to the ground.
Weakened by time and disease, its mighty trunk will fall.

I watch the man with spiked boots climb.
Ropes, pulley and chain saw in hand,
he slowly works his way up the trunk.

He saws, then lowers branches to the ground.
There, a chipper, grinding loudly,
quickly reduces debris to mulch.

Limbs gone, he works his way back down the mighty trunk,
sawing as he descends, until all that is left is a stump.
In less than a day, the tree has fallen.

Its profile and the seasonal beauty of its canopy are missed.
But mulch from its branches will blanket plants through
winter, and its logs will soon warm hearth and home.

Over time, with nurture, its seedling will grow,
until once again, a majestic giant will grace the landscape.

The Woodland Dragon

In Grandmother's garden out under the trees,
my dragon is sleeping, come, let's go and see.
He blew down with the wind a long time ago.
Just where he came from, I simply don't know.

A quite friendly dragon, not scary at all,
he really does like it when friends come to call.
He has big round eyes and a very long nose,
and a halo of horns, like a crown, I suppose.

His body is long and as smooth as can be,
with a kink near his tail, just under that tree.
But his wings are all broken and cannot be found.
That happened, I guess, when he fell to the ground.

When you run down his body, he'll fly, it is said,
if you hold real tight to the horns on his head.
I love that old dragon, and hope he will stay,
and not fly away on the next windy day.

Where Fairies Play

In Grandmother's garden on a sunny day,
I walked in the woods where the fairies play.

Magical merriment is under the trees
where fairies play, would you like to see?

Step very softly, make not a sound.
If they hear you, they cannot be found.

Just look on the ground where the shadows shift.
See, over there, watch the leaves start to lift.

FAIRIES!

Watch as they dance and frolic up on the log,
to the rhythm and cadence of birds and frogs.

On fluttering wings, feet leaving the ground,
see them jump and dance, not making a sound.

Watch them swirl and twirl, high up in the trees.
They bob and sway in the warm, gentle breeze.

With sun glittering on wings they take to the sky,
casting delicate shadows as they flit, then fly.

So Far Away, and Yet So Very Near

In the darkness, I gaze upward into a jet-black sky.
Lit by a sliver of moon, and peppered with stars,
it conjures memories, filling the void and
once again bringing light to my life.

Simplicity and Tranquility

Come sit a while in my garden swing,
put your worries away.
Sit quietly and attune your mind
to Mother Nature's day.

Turn the apps off, put that phone down.
The world will not end, no need to frown

Watch rabbits as they dine on tender sweet clover.
Hear the mocking bird's song, sung, over and over,
See the deer peacefully graze along with their fawn,
in the cool morning mist, out on the lawn.
Should the mist turn to rain, simply wander away-
misty memories, not worries now start your new day.

Christmas Pause and Ponder

It's the week before Christmas and here at our house,
we continue to scurry as quick as a mouse.
The trees are all trimmed, and the wreaths all hung,
but the house is a WRECK and the shopping not done!

As we panic and ponder, we try to make lists,
knowing full well we still need to get gifts.
No matter the scurry, no matter the crowds,
no matter the time, we all shout out loud.

For despite all the flurry, things will fall in place.
Gifts will be bought and smiles light each face.
So we pause and give thanks for the gifts we can't wrap,
as we ponder the pictures and cards in our laps.

We remember with fondness, friends old and new,
and give thanks for our blessings - for each one of you.
May your holiday be merry, your house filled with cheer,
and your walls ring with laughter throughout the New Year.

Father Time and Mother Nature

The wind that is blowing is no gentle breeze,
instead it has made my extremities freeze.

No doubt about it, that's PAIN that you see
in my ruby red cheeks and my creaky old knees.

My fingers are tingling and so are my toes,
I've begun to wonder about my nose.

It's still on my face, I know I can see it
The problem is I can't seem to feel it!

Layers of clothes just don't seem to matter,
old joints still creak and old bones still clatter.

So I'm turning around and heading back in.
Father Time, Mother Nature - I quit, you win!

Sights and Sounds of Fall

Sun glistens on dew-covered grass as a cool breeze shifts shadows on leaf covered ground, welcoming the arrival of fall.

Delightful sights and sounds greeted me on my trek through yard and woods.

Overhead, branches on the sweet gum swayed under the weight of transient cedar waxwings. Busily pecking on seedpods, they released a shower of tiny seeds for hungry ground sparrows.

The red headed woodpecker stopped its journey around the holly tree, when a flock of robins settled to gorge on its juicy red berries.

Overhead squirrels scurried, chattering displeasure at all interlopers.

Below, the gang of five crows convened and conversed at the feeder, then waddled their way to the birdbath for a drink.

I glanced up when the jay warned of the hawk's arrival.

Without a canopy of leaves, silence ensued and all movement stopped. until the hawk circled, dipped, and flew away.

Chattering and gorging resumed, I continued my sojourn, surrounded by and immersed in the glory of nature in fall.

The Spider's Lair

As I meandered through the trees…

That spider web I failed to see,
Soon became attached to me!
In my hair and on my glasses,
Stuck as if it were molasses.

Strands so fine, they were unseen,
Alas, now cloud my viewing screen.
Words of caution for what to see,
When next you stroll among the trees,

Look up, look down, look all around.
Don't always focus on the ground.
Or much like me, while unaware,
You'll find yourself in the spider's lair.

Observation

Today, I sat enjoying the warmth of the sun and a gentle breeze. Gazing at the shifting shadows of the woodland canopy, I watched a solitary leaf caught between branch and ground.

Defying gravity, it danced and spun endlessly on a single gossamer thread.

Kissed by the warm gentle breeze,
caught in a swirl of cascading leaves,
I paused, looked up, and gave thanks for the calm and serenity of this near perfect day.

The Poetry of Cynthia Frezek
Stardust

Cynthia Frezek wrote her first poem forty-five years ago on the subject of love and friendship. She published a small chapbook, Hearts in Transit.

Her career in nursing included oncology and palliative care as well as clinical education of the next generation of nurses. Recent poems reflect life experiences of aging and possibilities of finding deeper meaning in love and loss. She is a new member of James City Poets and resides in Williamsburg.

Atom Arrangement

"Every atom in our bodies was once a star" *

We start on rival tracks
And wind around steel trestle
Underbelly of birth

Picking up sand of rocks
Crushed DNA of centuries
Splashed seawater from Africa

Another perfect unfolding
Holding star power
Everlasting energy in a blast

Atom arrangement, a solo dance
In degrees of variation
Always newborn!

*Allan Sandage, Astronomer, 1926-2010

Celestial Sky

It stands in a crowd of many
Like a separate universe
Hot as desert wind
Silent for air to escape
Full of dreams to dance
In a black hole

Longing for quilts to cover
Days and hours, bleak wonder
Against the hook of lapsed
Months and calendar years
Stuck together on a branch
Destined to fall in unison

It holds burnt sage
Without ceremonial welcome

Pay Attention!

The journey from nowhere to not here unfolds

Old movies with Ginger Rogers dancing
Backwards in heels remind me
I was nowhere

As my parents laughed and loved
Precious leisure moments
Dancing through sad war loss
Draft moving separation trains
Telegrams of curt pasted words
Nightmare poems

No memory, only mystery
Surrounds breath
Grandmother's note,
"Babe has black hair like Bernie."
Loud cry set the journey in motion
Tears of joy and expectation

Characters in the welcome play
Are not here
I am nearly three quarters of a century
Into this timeline
Every day opens heart treasure
Clues to this passage

The journey from nowhere to not here continues

Pay Attention!

Stardust

Stardust emerged from piano keys
Under my mother's fingers
And I fell asleep
Heavenly melody after hours

On her last day I gazed
Transfixed on the hands
That held me first
Let me bang and smile music

Bones of her hands
Survive now in Stardust

Passing of Time

My father's end came twice
Once an accident
Undone by shock delivered
A snowy siren rescue
Interim unknown
And so the gift of time
Began again

I kept his watch

Minutes disappeared in clumps
Bound together
A mystery of swirling memories

My father reclaimed his watch at home

Time was running out
He checked hands
Hours, minutes

Kit took her watch

On a path known only to cats
A timepiece is no match for
Direct connection

My time arrived to witness breath last
And not another

I took his watch unwound

Memorial For a Friend

We are under the same sky
Circled by pinks and blues
Wandering clouds catching the last light
Now that the day warm easy time of love is gone
I search for common sights---you may be looking
At egrets, reflecting sunsets
Deflecting raindrops
Swimming and walking, humming and whispering
Writing me cosmic messages on the wind.

And painting, of course you would be painting
With all the rainbow colors in your heart
New shapes and shadows with you now
Dancing in another light---how can we
Span two worlds in the keeping and the taking
By Dog Star you opened me
Through the haze of tears around the moon
Into full silence, flowing over nothing

We had some practice at the creek
For no thingness flowing
Where can I find you when you've gone?
Look among the planets and the stars, you said.
Shall I sit in a bed of flowers to tell
Something wonderful I've read?
That might work too
Find me as you wish

Remembrances---trailing ribbon thread
Send a little humor twist so I'll know it's you.

Sacred Texts

The sea is full of sacred texts
Some are ancient and without words
All are hugged to a center
And then spewed out, crashing
Like an ugly lace over white sand

Talking death out of such announcements
Is futile, like hitting "Delete"
Only to find your message archived

Dead leaves of text ruffle
Along the edge of space time
My God, the sea is so aggressive!
It shocks cold words to tears

I Can Imagine a New Nothing in the Universe

I can imagine a new nothing in the universe
With all the beeps and alarms of ICU
Tangled vines of tubing
Not in anyone's trail dreams

And yet it is a path
The road you must take
Kicking and screaming with clenched teeth
Or like a faint smile of window screen breeze

Out of rubble all dust particles gather
For the long journey above birds to stars
Original home, if you like (or not)
Preparation optional

Have you not studied miraculous flowers
Soon transformed in Fall
Gathered forces for estranged good-byes
Somewhere along the last ribbon tethered to earth

I have witnessed water from the Ganges River
Bless the deceased
And the medicine man dance a plan of care
Yes, I pulled the rubber band until it snapped
Revealing white pelicans and hot air balloons
By the thousands
Nothing imagined, everything unexpected

Mountain Dreams

Places in my heart
For sitting still
Wrapped around you
So quick

The slip of an angel twist
Into the pocket of my being
Love comes up in me over you
Spilling through seams

You found my undercover soul
Driftwood from the night wind
No finer wings for me than folded

Deep down in your body for blessing
And none but the darkest cave
Promise a song

Preserve Our Woods!

Chinese dragon dazzling color
Frightens all the white tailed deer
The stately redwood wisely sings
A mantra joyful magic near
A space to play

Birds of freedom give the young
Protection in the night
When daunting circumstances rise
To streak the sky with beads of light
A storm today

Trucks and men drag muddy tools
Destruction under high top boots
Tiny creatures seek to hide
Amid the stark remains of roots
"We'd like to stay!"

Prophesy

Prophesy---soul clock work
An arching snow panther
Chasing the night bird of Spring

Sand explosion in life's upheaval
Pouring down gentle honey space for love
Heart songs in longing find their time

Final truth is living out all wonder
Spilling rivers penetrate the deep
Feelings of beauty hidden clearly alive

Flight swirl in sky smoke rings
Engraving on memory alone
The permanence of wings

Falling

Maybe that's it
I never learned how to fall
Gracefully, that is
My parachute fails to open
No drifting peacefully for long
Just plunging to the ground
Even a yo-yo escapes that fate
By hanging on a string
Up and down

Feathered Gatherings

How would it be without words
If we were all birds
Free to share the air and care
About ruffled feathers together

I could tell you in silence
That I have gone to sea
And filled joyfully with life
Some purpose beneath the surface

Shared many a morsel from captains' tables
And stretched in flight as far as I am able
Then again my beach is miles of sand
An empty walk holding no one's hand

Like the night bird minds the light
So it will be now as I take flight
Words are lost to the ocean breeze
Our memory comforts in many new trees

Still Out There

What path for the journey?
Which bend in the road?
A twist of starlight, shadow trees
And green, there must be green
Newness on which to focus light within

Upstream under mist and mountain
Colorful melodies dance a flame
Wind dries tears in trickles
Warming spray of the fountain

A marathon of hearts
Touch down in quietness
Depth and forever movements
Stir in my soul, trusting
River current on which I grow

Rock danced and free
Join me

The Poetry of Edward W. Lull
And Life Goes On

Edward Lull grew up in Upstate New York, and graduated from the U.S. Naval Academy. He earned a master's degree from The George Washington University in 1969. After his Navy career, Lull held management and executive positions in several small hi-tech firms in the Washington, D.C. area.

Lull began writing poetry in retirement; he published six books of his poetry: Cabin Boy to Captain: a Sea Story in 2003, Where Giants Walked in 2005, The Sailors: Birth of a Navy in 2007, Bits and Pieces: A Memoir in 2011, Creating Form Poetry in 2013, and The Reality and Fantasy of My World in 2017. He is a Life Member in the Poetry Society of Virginia and served four terms as its president. He chairs the James City Poets workshop.

My Oval Landscape

The stands are board-hard, unforgiving seats
where anxious parents, friends, and fans collect
to watch and cheer for track athletes who know
that head and legs and heart must now connect.

Like most, I have my stopwatch in my hands;
my eyes are focused on the starter's gun.
One can't rely on sound - it's just too slow;
my thumb awaits the flash to start the run.

* *

Her blonde hair, pony-tailed, flew arrow-straight
then bobbed in sync with obstacles below.
With picture form, she soared with grace and ease;
no hurdles in her lane received a blow.
This little girl knew her success required
agility and speed, not strength and size.
At race's end, she wore the winning tape,
then on the platform, claimed her golden prize.

   No natural athlete was this fair-skinned boy
   who trained as hard as any I had seen.
   Exhausting workouts soon produced results
   as PRs came to be almost routine.
   At six feet, lean, he had an upright style
   and loved to run in front and lead the pack.
   He left his school the middle distance king;
   the one who looked ahead and never back.

      A skilled performer in 'most any sport,
      he tried the track to see if he would fit.
      No burning speed, he chose the distance runs:
      success defined by stamina and grit.
      Cross country soon became his running forte;
      he trained on hills in weather cold and damp,
      but he was well-prepared for his big race.
      This harrier became the county champ.

* *

That generation all became adults
so many years ago - but in my mind
the scenes are just as clear as if they were
the movies of my dreams I could rewind.

The thrill of competition is renewed,
with nervousness I hardly can ignore.
As children of my children toe the line,
my oval landscape comes alive once more.

55 at Fifty

(A tribute to the USNA Class of 1955 on its 50th reunion)

From all across the forty-eight, we came
and gathered in July of fifty-one.
Harry Truman was our leader's name;
Korea's war was far from being done.

For four long years we struggled to become
the type of leaders people would respect.
On Graduation Day we would succumb
to heady dreams of lives we might expect.

We soon learned leaders need to be inspired
before they're proven worthy of their stripes.
We imitated those that we admired,
but found we really had no prototypes.

As individuals we made our way
through complex mazes each of us would face.
As time went on, some heard the call to say
"farewell" - and other ventures they'd embrace.

Regardless of the field, there was success,
and heartbreak every time we took a loss.
Our fallen classmates forced us to address
the omnipresence of the albatross.

Now fifty years since when we tossed our caps,
embarking on a life we barely knew,
we still get misty-eyed when we hear taps,
and "Blue and Gold" excites our hearts anew.

We sailed the seven seas and flew the skies,
and fought our country's battles on the ground.
Our classmates passed life's tests with steady eyes;
adventures that we sought we surely found.

When age and wisdom seem to coincide,
we realize our work was not in vain.
Whatever role we played, we could take pride;
we'd been a link in that unbroken chain.

An Epiphany

"I doubt that she'll last the night,"
the doctor murmured in hushed tone
and closed the door behind him.
Drugs assured that she'd sleep in peace,
undisturbed by tortuous pain she had endured
these past few months.
The death watch is a painful duty
most never are called to perform.

Sitting quietly, musing over the highlights
of her life - I saw her hand move.
Quickly by her side, I saw her eyes open,
a look of concern apparent. It was like
she had a sudden conscious thought
that penetrated the haze; she had forgotten
something and wanted to make it right.
I believe she would have gotten up - but she couldn't.

My brother arrived to relieve me as agreed.
I went home, tired, and looking forward
to a restful night. After brushing my teeth,
I donned my pajamas and slipped beneath
the covers. In a light doze, I suddenly
startled awake. I wondered:
Had I locked the back door?
Had I turned off the garage light?
Had I turned down the thermostat?

I had to check, so I got up - because I could.
Returning to bed, I considered
parallels and differences
between her night and mine.
It brought new understanding
of Joseph Awad's poem, Night Thoughts:
"Sleep is a rehearsal for our dying;
Each awakening a mini-resurrection."

Resolution

(Upon Retirement)

My days of working to survive
have passed me by, so what comes now?
Is this unending holiday?
Is this the rest life will allow?

Does my retirement stop my brain
or still my search for life's surprise?
I hardly think I can deny
my brain or body exercise.

God did not put me here to watch
and wait for strength and skill to fade.
To put my skills to use each day
brings joy that I cannot evade.

So let these aging years pile up,
I'll not surrender to their threat.
As will and energy still live,
I'll journey on without regret.

Ode To A Gnat

To mow my lawn in Spring should be
a task that I would not oppose.
However, all tranquility
is dashed; a gnat flew up my nose!

My tiny friend, you know you are
a pest I wish would disappear.
Just when I think you've gone afar,
you dare to buzz in my left ear.

You are so small I have no clue
if you're a Mr. or a Mrs.
Nor do I care, when all you do
is clog my facial orifices.

What do you do here, anything
besides annoy us friendly folk?
There is no joy I see you bring
when down my throat you make me choke.

Perhaps you're here to feed a bird;
your only use: to serve as food.
So flying in my eye's absurd
and won't improve my nasty mood.

If bird food is its total use,
I'll make a deal with these my terms:
Destroy all gnats, and then produce
a bumper crop of juicy worms!

And Life Goes On

Sixteen Soldiers Killed on Weekend,
the headline shouted, begging to be noticed.
The article went on describing carnage
caused by car bomb and sniper fire.

> In his freshly-pressed suit and starched collar
> the man entered the kitchen, fixed his coffee,
> and sat down at the breakfast table.

Passers-by walked on
while brave men lay dying in the street.

> Slipping the sports page out,
> he tossed the rest of the paper aside
> and began his careful study
> of Sunday's football results.

A picture showed a soldier,
draped from his vehicle,
oozing life.
An alert photographer had done his job
before disgorging.

> Having completed this daily ritual
> he arose, put cup and saucer in the sink.
> "I'll be a little late," he called,
> "Handball with Peter tonight."
> Then left for work.

Face-down on the table
remained the paper with its chilling words:
Sixteen Soldiers Killed on Weekend.

The Time For Change

What makes a politician what he is?
When are his ideals suctioned from his head?
What makes him reach for things that just aren't his?
Who fills that trough to see that he is fed?

The Constitution says how they should play,
but lawmakers can bend the rules at will.
Their run for reelection starts the day
they take the oath; their futures to fulfill.

They also promise things they can't control,
and act like friends with people they can't stand.
Their speeches could replace my Demerol
with metaphors we all misunderstand.

Do you support incumbent's plaintive pleas
when he brings federal money to your zone?
Is that called statesmanship - or a disease
that we, the voters, openly condone?

They call it pork - but it's to buy your vote,
and Congress greets it with a wink and nod.
However, they condemn the budget's bloat,
"Let's cut the pork!" an often-heard façade.

Our legislators have become the slaves
of party, large contributors, and greed.
Decisions made in private, small conclaves
are seldom aimed at meeting nation's need.

Both parties' leaders - not by accident,
have yielded to the arrogance of power.
Their voting party lines - embarrassment:
but going against their party makes them cower!

Since soft campaign funds help them to succeed,
to pay off obligations is a must.
It seems that they no longer need to heed
that public service is a public trust.

I hardly think reform will be a goal
of those who sit in judgment on themselves.
A bill that might upset a leader's role
will find its final place on dusty shelves.

I know that we cannot begin anew
and form a system that would make more sense -
for instance, one where red states might turn blue,
and blue turn red based on the year's events.

Hello, you voters, when will you decide
that you, at last, have had enough of this?
The problems, we can see, are country-wide;
if we ignore them, are we not remiss?

Those there the longest should be first to go
so leadership can pass to newer hands.
Careers in Congress are not apropos;
complacency will not meet our demands.

Since we have means to make a peaceful change
what makes us sit and let this cancer grow?
It's frustrating, and yes it's even strange
that we would just accept the status quo.

So what will your response to these words be?
Perhaps a few of you may write a letter.
But honestly I wrote it all for me;
unloading it on you makes me feel better!

A Lesson Learned

It was bottom of the ninth, two outs,
Wally on third, Mike on second.
Jonathan, the tall right-hander,
had worked the count on me to two-and-two.
We had been ahead 4-3 after eight,
but my error in the top of the ninth
cost us two unearned runs.

I backed off from the plate to take a breath.
Jonathan had his stuff today;
he had worked the inside corner effectively,
getting me to take one and foul off another.
With one ball to give, where will he go?
I'm betting he'll try to slip one
on the outside corner around the knees.
* * *
It was the day after school had let out;
Mom let me have a little party at home.
Things got a bit raucous. Billy spilled his soda;
Jackson knocked over a full bowl of pop corn.
When Mom came home, the boys left.
Mom looked around and in a soft but firm voice said:
"This is your mess; clean it up."
* * *
The incident flashed through my mind:
this was my mess to clean up.
I took my stance, ready.
After his stretch and getting his signals,
Jonathan checked the runners;
I edged an inch or two closer to the plate.
The pitch was wide but waist high;
I launched it over the second baseman's head
to right center. Wally and Mike scored,
a walk-off single. Thanks, Mom!

Coincidental Metaphor

My walking path led me
   through light woods and brush.
     Six feet off the trail lay
       the lifeless form of a rabbit,
body untouched, but headless.

A predator had killed and decapitated,
   not in self defense,
     not to fill a hunger need,
       but just because he could;
it was his nature.

To my left, a movement drew my attention.
   A turkey vulture lurked
     in the brush, awaiting my departure
       to approach without risk
and pick clean the victims bones.

War's like that:
   predators,
     victims,
       vultures,
         observers,
and sudden, violent death.

A Squirrel's Lament

As I was on my walk today
a rodent whined at me.
It was a sad, yes mournful sound
emerging from the tree.

I've had them yell at me before
but this was really weird.
I glanced up to a low branch where
the furry guy appeared.

He sat erect, his head held high,
his tail a question mark.
So what is this lament about:
his love life lacking spark?

Perhaps he lost his girl friend and
that made his spirits sag.
When zipping 'cross the street below
she zigged when she should zag.

Do squirrels cry when they are sad
and shed real tears of woe?
With all of them that live right here
I think that I should know.

So then I thought a toothache caused
the furry fellow's drear.
Regretting now he hadn't seen
his dentist twice a year.

Could nervous stomach be to blame,
and not his teeth at all?
I wondered if he'd get relief
from phenobarbital.

I'm onto something here that caused
that strange, pathetic chirp.
It wasn't lost love after all;
he needed just to burp.
* * *
I walk about three miles a day,
good time to just reflect.
But stupid rodent thoughts will not
improve my intellect.

The Leader is ...

the one they look to when they've lost their way,
the one who raises spirits when they're down,
the one who will go back to help a stray,
the one who leads, but never wears a crown,

the one who will endure the daily pain,
the one who will provide the needed spark,
the one who works for good, not just for gain,
the one who finds the light amid the dark,

the one who stands apart, though in a crowd,
the one who will solve problems that arise,
the one who always speaks the truth aloud,
the one who will support, not criticize,

the one who listens to another's view,
the one who lives with energy and verve,
the one who will commit and follow through.
The leader is the one who's called to serve.

The False Start

It simply wasn't meant to be,
my game of golf today.
A storm with lightning flashes caused
a two-hour-long delay.

This was the only day this week
that I could play a round.
I didn't want to miss the chance
because of soggy ground.

At last, the starter sent us out;
the first tee box was soft.
My foot slipped when I swung my club;
the ball had little loft

and landed near the ladies' tee,
just twenty yards in all.
My second shot, a fairway wood,
addressed the muddy ball.

A fairly decent shot, I thought,
of course no bounce or roll.
My next shot I could hope to reach
the green on this first hole.

While choosing which club I should use
a clap of thunder broke
my concentration, startling all;
I couldn't take my stroke.

Course rules required that we return
at once to starter's shack.
He greeted us with: "Sorry, guys,
the storm is coming back."

We waited just a little while
enough time for a beer,
but rain kept coming down and clouds
refused to disappear.

And so twelve clubs still in my bag
I never got to use.
I trudged on home, put clubs away,
and cleaned my muddy shoes.

The Ballad of Deliverance

or

Dropping a Daughter Off at College

"Sunny, hot, and humid" blared
the radio upstairs.
This August date I hardly cared,
so wrapped up in my prayers.

The year - a long, long time ago,
our daughter was, at last,
packing for the trip, you know,
the time has gone so fast.

Acceptance at her school of choice
seemed wonderful in June;
I hardly think I shall rejoice
this summer afternoon.

A loaded car; it's time to go,
for Williamsburg we're bound.
The conversation seemed to flow,
but we were tightly wound.

The temperature was ninety-four
when we reached Barrett Hall.
"I'll carry stuff, you get the door,"
"Be careful not to fall."

Unloading took an hour plus,
the sweat was flowing free.
Twas then the roommates greeted us,
I was a sight to see.

Parents talked and roommates shared;
"That one's an extrovert."
We wondered if she were prepared;
my head began to hurt.

One roommate asked, "What's your I.Q.?"
My stomach churned a bit.
The time to leave had come, I knew,
there's no avoiding it.

Goodbyes are hard and always lead
to tears and trite expression.
We cannot bring the depth we need
to offset the depression.

We drove off, left our pride, our joy,
defenseless, as it were.
"I hope you saw that dark haired boy!
The way he looked at her!"

My wife was silent then for good,
a tear leaked from her eye.
We knew we'd done the best we could;
she'd earned her wings to fly.

The Legacy

Her glancing blow that stole
the sunshine from the Sunshine State
left us with almost casual thought:
another nasty storm.
But in the days ahead she became full-grown,
salivating over her next victim;
she took her time to savor what would come.
Dreaming of her name in history books,
she attacked the most defenseless prey.

Warnings went unheeded:
"After all we handled *Camille*, didn't we?"
The poor, when told to go, did not know where,
or if they did, lacked the means to get there.
Lashing winds made buildings dance
before collapsing into matchsticks.
The Gulf engulfed all that dared to dare.
Land, life and livelihood succumbed.

Before departing, she fired
one more lethal shot
to elevate herself from common killer
to epic mass murderer.
As dikes were breached when she moved north,
water flooded south.
The sight of death afloat is etched
forever in our minds.
We have no power to evacuate
images of dismal decomposing death:
Katrina's legacy.

Mercury

*...achieving the goal, before this decade is out, of landing a man on the moon
and returning him safely to the earth. ... J.F. Kennedy, May 25, 1961*

While cameras clicked to capture Alan's smile,
he crawled into his saucer-shaped cocoon.
His mission was the perilous first step
that could someday land man upon the moon.

No matter what the outcome, it was clear:
succeed or fail, the journey wouldn't last.
The gentle landing in the Navy's realm
provided sharp contrast to lift-off's blast.

When Gus shot off, the confidence was high;
but still, the awesome lift-off gave us pause.
As parachute deployed we breathed a sigh,
another mission ending without flaws.

However, bobbing in the waves disturbed
the spaceman's stomach and he felt quite ill.
He was extracted but his coffin sank;
this day would not his destiny fulfill.

The final, longer flight belonged to John;
his mission - gird the globe, then back to earth.
The images displayed enthralled us all;
successes of the program proved its worth.

As later tragedies would demonstrate
the risks that such a daring program brings.
We must salute these brave men who allowed
the goal that JFK proclaimed take wings.

The Poetry of Peggy Newcomb
Down Mountain Laurel Lane

Peggy Newcomb has a BS degree in chemistry from Mary Washington College of the University of Virginia.

She taught chemistry and science at York High School, Yorktown, Virginia. She has written for several news-papers and has been published in several venues including the Poet's Domain.

She was awarded first place for non-fiction in the Chesapeake Bay Writer's Conference. She is a member of the National League of American Pen Women and the James City Poets. She lives in Gloucester, Va.

Wedding Memories

On the beach a bamboo altar
built by her father
stands tall.
A gentle breeze caresses the shore,
the white tulle billows gracefully in a
dance of love…bringing back
memories of a special day:
my daughter's wedding.

Two sons give their mother's hand in marriage.
One beams with pride. The other,
the family comedian,
sheds a tear of nostalgia.

The groom (his son by his side)
proudly stands under the canopy of
blue sky and quietly sheds tears of happiness
as his bride approaches the beach.

The maid of honor, the groom's teenage daughter, sobs.
She's waited for this moment with
anxious anticipation for several years
and can't believe it's finally here.

Above, a seagull floats on an upward draft.
The clouds, a fluffy white, slowly drift
across that vibrant blue sky.

The scene is lovely.
The crowd…joyful.
The bride… beautiful.
The couple… beaming.
The parents …hopeful that these adults
have found true love at last.

The tulle flutters gently in the breeze.
The couple is pronounced husband and wife.
"Now you may kiss the bride."
The music starts and so does:
Life, Hope and Joy.

Jesus wasn't there but
the water did turned into wine.
Or was he?

Who Wants To Listen To the Clock?

My house could be neat with everything in place.
But it's not.
There are papers on the floor, crayons on the table,
and shoes piled at the door.

Little feet come running through,
"Nana, where are you?" they shout!
In the kitchen on the porch or
somewhere near about.

I wouldn't have it any other way.
Tick.. .Tock.. .Tick.. .Tock.
Who wants to listen to the clock?
Neat and clean can be awful lonely.

I'd rather have Kool-Aid, Gator Aid, or
lemonade running down the counter,
sand on the floor, cookies baking in the oven,
water running in the tub or
voices scrapping over who walks the dog.

I actually like bandages,
Mercurochrome, and
chocolate covered Oreo lips!

I love questions like:
What do you have to eat?
What can we make? or
Can I spend the night?

"Let's go out on the boat..
I want to go fishing!" my grandson shouts.
Shove the boat away from the dock!

Who wants to listen to the clock?

My Trip To Wonderland

As I sat with my eyes closed
And as the music played
A rabbit hopped
From out the woods.
It was a lovely day.
He had a gift, was in a box
Tied tightly with a bow.

He looked at me
And twitched his nose
As only rabbits can
and continued to nudge his gift
slowly across the lawn.

A little girl who next appeared
Was clutching her fabric doll.
Warm and cozy in her arms
It's what she holds so dear.

She hides the doll when mother comes
Who wants to throw it out
But the doll is more than just a doll
It's been with her since birth.

A beautiful bird lights nearby
But never comes to stay
And when the young girl approaches it
It swiftly flits away.

Perhaps its love that's in the box
Tied tightly with a bow.

The rabbit next a teddy bear brings
With a heart held in its hand
Take the heart he says and search for
Truth while you're in Wonderland.

Perhaps its love that's in the box
Tied tightly with a bow.

As I sit and watch the scene
My heart begins to ache
For the child with clutching doll
Whose longing for her mother's love
Has always seen heartbreak.

The tears I shed
Were from my heart
For the child I've raised and love
She has my love
But it does not fill
The hole that's in her soul.

Perhaps its love that's in the box
Tied tightly with a bow.

The gift is pushed toward the child
To untie the bow
For the time has come
to accept the love from
the family that you know.
Allow this love to mend your soul
And help your heart to grow.

Yes, love was in the rabbit's box
Tied tightly with a bow.

February 14th

The sweetest thing I've ever seen on Valentine's Day
I saw this morning while l was driving my
granddaughter to school. We were five minutes later
than usual so the middle school bus we usually follow
with its frequent stops had moved on and
we sailed down the winding road uninterrupted.

The morning air was crisp, the mist was rising off
the frost covered fields as the sun was sending
its yellow beams through the trees.
My granddaughter was playing her favorite
music station on the radio…..
"It started with a whisper… then I kissed her".

It was about this time that we realized the
high school students were standing outside
waiting for their bus to arrive.

"Oh, look over there!" my granddaughter shouted.
"There's a high school student holding a huge
teddy bear! How sweet!" she beamed …
thinking of the lucky girl who would be surprised
this morning at school by her boyfriend.

I could only think that he must really be in love
to face the jeers of the other boys on the bus and
in the halls while carrying that large teddy bear.
I found myself picturing the scene in my mind
as we zipped along.

Then Alexis shouted," Oh, look, Nana!
He has flowers." And sure enough at the next
bus stop stood a tall baby faced young man
dressed in a suit and tie, his books in one hand
and a lovely nosegay of flowers in the other.

I so wished I could have taken a picture
of the two students. Not knowing it,
they brought back the sweet memories of
the stolen kiss, the passionate embrace,
the thrill of love and the excitement of being in love.

Remembering these moments made my Valentine's Day.

Who Wrote This Play?

The water's on for coffee.
I can hear the sizzling sound.
The dog and cat roam the house
looking all around.

The flowers on the table
are fading slowly as I
sit here all alone.

I miss my husband, my lover, my friend.
I want him here by my side.

For fifty years we've shared this life,
through happy times and sad.
To face it all alone
doesn't seem quite fair.

I miss our fireside chats every morning,
sipping coffee as our granddaughter
prepared for school.

I miss lying next to him
and listening to him breathe.
I miss the good night kiss he always
gave me on my left cheek.

"I love you, Honey." I'd say.
"I love you too." Came his reply
before we fell asleep.

Now it's me, the dog, and the cat
wishing for our friend.
It wasn't suppose to be this way.
Who wrote this play?

Checkpoint Charlie Museum, Berlin

I saw pictures of ingenious escapes
 of loved ones rescuing one another
 of mothers never being reunited with their children and

I cried.

I saw paintings depicting helplessness,
powerlessness, desperation and despair and

I cried.

I saw pictures of the wall, of failed attempts to break free,
of people shot and left to slowly bleed to death in the
 death zone.

I saw windows filled with bricks and concrete,
 the wall being reinforced and
a father holding up his son to view the world beyond.
I felt a hollow empty place inside.

I saw men called God give speeches and order down the
 wall.
I heard the music play and the people cheer.
I had witnessed the price of freedom and

I cried.

The Back Porch

One day a brick mason showed up at my home
to lay the foundation for the back porch.
The contractor had already dug the trench and
poured the concrete footing.

As we walked around the side of the house and
arrived at the back, he asked,
"What exactly is this addition going to be?"

At my feeble attempt to be funny and
in my exaggerated southern accent I said,
"It's going to be a veranda."

I was embarrassed when he asked,
"What is a veranda?"
"Oh, I was just being silly." I replied.
"That's a southern word for back porch."

"Oh." he said as he proceeded to do his work.

A month or so later he returned to lay the steps
after the porch had been completed.
There were four square white columns in place and
a mahogany floor gleaming
with a fresh coat of protectorate
and no furniture to mar the view.

As the brick mason rounded the end of the house
he stopped as his eye caught a glimpse
of the nearly completed porch.

"Wow!" he exclaimed, "It is a veranda!"

Gardens

I've seen the gardens at Versailles,
the impressive beds of red and yellow blooms
at Buckingham Palace,
the quiet lovely courtyard at Potsdam.

But, my garden lies within the woods…
with pink Lady Slippers,
Ragweed, Queen Anne's Lace and
the red berries of the Wintergreen plant.

With flowing stream
and bending oak
and large boulders basking
in the sun of a spring day.

It's a mountain trail with
red and yellow leaves gently
fluttering to the ground…
and the smell of nature all around.

It's a place to rest,
to recreate.
It fills my heart with joy
and my eyes with tears that
take me back to days gone by.

This to me is God's Garden
and it speaks to my soul.

Looking Forward Through a Rear View Mirror

I came face to face with my mortality:
a mammogram, a biopsy, a mastectomy.
"Don't worry." they said, "Only 15% are malignant."
Not so for me. Now my breast is gone.
I cried and felt sorry for myself.

But I'm still alive."If thine eye offends thee, pluck it out."
Mark 9:47 No doubt that's the thing to do,
but emotionally it's hard.

As pre-adolescent girls we wait for our figures to bloom,
so we can look like the older girls, the movie stars,
the bathing beauties on TV. And now, they come
with scalpel and knife and lop it off…my breast!...and say:
"Oh well. Take these pain pills if needed."

But what about the pain in my mind, behind my eyes
that fills up and spills over? What about the nights
when my brain won't cut off and I think about death
and I wonder: Is my time here and now?
Will I suffer? Has it spread? They said they got it all.

"Now let's go after any microscopic cells that may be
inside your body."But where? Where are they lurking?
If we only knew.

I feel good. I've recovered from the surgery. I want
To get on with my life. Do I walk on eggshells?
Always wondering?

"Take your chemo," my daughter says, "and live your life.
None of us knows what tomorrow may bring."

I read in the literature that you'll never live life the same.
You'll appreciate every breath you take, every raindrop,
every sunny day, every birdcall.

I was feeling weepy while driving my three year old
granddaughter to pre-school. From the back seat I heard
that angel's voice say:"I"(said very drawn out).That's the
signal for me to repeat what she's just said…..so I say…
(very drawn out) …."I"

"Lo-ove."She says.

"Lo-ove. "I repeat.

"You."

"You."

I adjust the rear view mirror and soak up the rays
coming from that precious face and
forget my tears!

The Reunion

They were somebody, they were nobody.
A fleeting smile, a flicker of memory.
Will I recognize them?
What year is this?
2013, fifty years!
Where have they gone?

I was busy! Doing what?
Do I remember?
Well…teaching school, raising children,
 juggling schedules, buying groceries,
 washing dishes, clothes.
But fifty years worth? It couldn't be.

Wasn't it only yesterday when we parted
wishing everyone good luck and success?
And now? And now we meet again.
How will they look? How do I look?
What have you been doing?
Did we grow? Are we better?
Wiser?More confident? Assured?

Tell me your name again.
Maybe fifty years has been a long time.
Do you know me?

I'm not the same you know. I've
thought new thoughts, made decisions,
lost a parent, a friend, a child.

I've weathered storms you'll
never know I weathered because
I won't tell you about them, but they
left their mark just the same.

I've hurt more than I thought possible.
Cried until there were no more tears.
Felt powerless and alone.
And I've loved!
I've laughed and I've experienced
the joy that comes from years of struggle.

Gosh, a lot has happened. Hasn't it?

When we meet, will our hearts meet
and share the depth or will this be another
"don't tell me too much" cocktail party?

Tell me your name again.
Do I know you?

Thoughts While Listening To a Classical Concert

The notes float through the room
on a butterfly's wing.
Asking
what of us?
To hear and to enjoy…
but maybe more?

There it is again.
The music in full volume and strength,
determined to fill the hall.
Driving its message home with the speed of a racing train.
Again and again the notes are repeated.
They seem to say:
Here we are!
Here is life!
Here!
Here!
Now!

Taking the listener on a roller coaster ride or
tiptoeing quietly through a forest.

Then a harmonic tone
transforms my mind
to think about the
rising and falling of the waves.
It gently moves like a musical ribbon
winding its way through the air.
Now resounding with power
off the walls and into our hearts.
Such intensity
never heard before.

Is there a message in the music?
What twists and turns it seems to take
intertwining with the other instruments
in a dance of life.

There's that intensity again and again,
A light note and then back to dread!
The musicians play on.
Where will it end?

Yesteryear

"Yesteryear"
reminds me of when every spare
piece of land in
Gloucester was planted in daffodils.

My husband, as a boy,
grew up at White Marsh and remembers
picking and packing daffodils
into boxes until midnight
when trucks would stop
to pick up the boxes
and take them to Washington D.C.,
Baltimore and even New York City.

The flowers bloomed earlier down south
but without refrigerator trucks
they could not get the blooms
to the big cities before they wilted.

Leaving Gloucester at midnight
meant the daffodils could be
on the city streets by morning,
bobbing their yellow heads in the sunshine
of a cool spring day.

What Is Christmas?

Christmas to me is a joyous season.
Christmas is caroling.
It's the smell of turkey and sweet potato pie
baking in the oven.
It's the glitter of lights on the tree. the smell of pine
and the beauty of holly on the table….
The crackle of wood burning in the fireplace.

Christmas is a child's excited
anticipation of what Santa will bring.
Christmas is celebrating love of family
and the appreciation of friends around the table
or over a cup of good cheer.

Christmas is a time to show gratitude for our blessings.
A time to share our blessings with others.
A time to spend a quiet moment
in church or some special place
to thank God for the Christ child…
our reason for Christmas.

Perhaps our prayer should be to spread
the spirit of Christmas throughout the year.

The Poetry of Adele Richards Oberbelman
Reflections

Adele Richards Oberhelman, a Pennsylvania native and retired Executive Secretary/Administrator, worked for the Aluminum Company of America in Pittsburgh; the U. S. Army Aviation Material Laboratories at Fort Eustis, Virginia; and Anheuser-Busch, Inc. in Williamsburg, Virginia. Over the years, Adele has written poetry from time to time, but not in any concentrated way until she joined the James City Poets. A resident of Williamsburg and Montebello, she has one son who lives with his wife in the mountains of central Virginia.

Decline

Her hair's unkempt, eyes vacant
  as the house next door.
When did she come to realize
  there never would be more?
Her thoughts return to early days,
  when kids were very young.
She tried to keep them clean and
  fed, while to her skirts they clung.
She worked two jobs to pay the rent;
  to keep them off the street.
Sometimes she'd take in laundry,
  just to make ends meet.

The children grew, then went away,
  seldom to return.
The neighborhood became rundown,
  some structures left to burn.
Her once neat home is dingy now;
  she can't afford the soap.
She can't work those long hours now;
  she's given up all hope.

It's difficult for her, these days,
  to make it up the stairs.
But worse, she's come to realize
  that no one really cares.
How can she even contemplate
  her few remaining years
when all that looms before her are
  the specters that she fears.

We've judged her by our standards,
  with little empathy
or understanding that she was
  the best that she could be.

My Father's Garden

Walking with my father, through his garden,
I only saw the flowers.
It hadn't then occurred to me
great love was in the hours
that he spent there, in evenings,
with hands deep in the soil,
or what those hours meant to him,
a respite from day's toil.

A quiet, earnest, working-man,
those flowers were his pleasure.
I now look back upon those walks
as time to truly savor.
We didn't speak of feelings as
we passed a special tree,
but sharing time among his plants
assured me he loved me.

He nurtured more than flowers
with his caring, giving ways
leaving me with memories of sun-filled happy days.
We often strolled that special ground
where his flowers grew;
I loved him then, as I do still….
although unspoken, I hope he knew.

Time Limit (on Grief)

We scream inside;
but, we're civilized
and cannot let it show

We learn to deal with visceral grief;
there's sympathy,
though it's all too brief

There's "a time to grieve",
 the pundits say,
 then we must -- "let it go"

We must don a smile,
put the tears away,
for they really don't want to know.

Live Long and Prosper

I've loved you since before your birth.
Live long and prosper on this earth!

Enjoy its colors, sounds, and spheres
and wear the mantle of your years
in wisdom, wonder, searching awe,
while ferreting the secrets of
this earth and all the worlds beyond,
the depths within, the ongoing song
of life well-lived and often savored.

Enjoy success of one most favored
with a special intellect,
with a reverence and respect
for all the things of earth and sea,
of time and space....eternity....
discovery of that which is,
and revelations yet to be.

But most of all, know your own worth.
Live long and prosper on this earth!

    I've loved you since
    before your birth.

The First Moon Landing

(that we know of)
July 20, 1969

'Twas a special day in history,
that day in '69
A small step for a man;
a leap for all mankind

They'd gone where no one had before
Bill watched, though he was only four

He checked another channel
Much to his dismay,
he learned his friend, Deputy Dog,
was in need of aid

He aimed his trusty pistol at the villain in the plot
A stream of water sliced its way toward that very spot

The shot from Bill's small water gun
arced down to hit a tube
He knew, from the resulting "pop"
that he'd wiped out that rube

We learned, but not from TV,
man HAD landed on the moon.
Bill would see "The Dog" another day
but Mom hoped not too soon

Dream Catcher

You sort and sift my dreams while I'm asleep,
permitting only pleasant dreams to pass.
But what of buried dreams,
or those I never dared to dream,
could those come through a smoky looking-glass?

Through tangled webs of obstacles and thoughts
beyond minutia of the day to day,
Can you catch hazy dreams from deep inside,
those buried before ever fully forming,
capture them to bring to me at first light
then hold dream power for me in the morning?

Exotic, Erotic Artichokes

(An Artichoke Heart)

The painting of artichokes evoked such feeling.
I vividly remember the first time I ate one.
You introduced me to that pleasure.

I watched you become immersed in their preparation,
placing garlic, herbs and wine in water to steam them,
clarifying and seasoning butter in which to dip the leaves.

We sipped champagne while they were steaming.
When ready, you invited me to participate in the ritual:
remove one leaf at a time,
dip it,
strip the tasty pulp with my teeth.

You watched me, hoping I was savoring this treat as much as you.
....dipping....stripping....savoring....
Finally, the piece de resistance,
 the heart:
 cut apart,
     dip and savor.

Consuming this exotic treat was an almost erotic experience.
You were so generous of spirit,
taking pleasure in my enjoyment of new things.

The artichoke is now, for me,
a metaphor for the many layers that made the person that was you,
    my heart,
      cut apart.

My Child

Precious child, unlined of brow, in sweet repose
I gaze on your untroubled sleep, so good.
The fragrance of your hair, fresh from the wood.

The sleep of youth, unfettered and so free
The searching of the young for that which "is,"
as yet unbound by that which "ought to be."

Grant me the wisdom that I may direct
yet not to try to mold to ways I know.
Rather to provide the means to learn
to set your wondrous spirit free to grow.

Who knows what marv'lous truths you may foretell,
what glories of your spirit may unfurl.
I hope to guide you wisely for a while
that you may know the world; yourself as well.

Consider the Crow

Consider the crow, with his
beady eye,
his coarse black feathers,
with shine so high.

While multi-colored songbirds sing
and butterflies are fluttering,
he's busy just remembering
the treats that dawn will often bring.

He watches from a far off tree
and scans the fertile field to see
if danger lurks there for his friends;
on his sharp eyes the flock depends.

He calls to let his comrades know
it's safe for them to come and go.
The owner of the farm's away
so this becomes a crows' feast day.

The Difference

The sun still rises in the east
delivering a visual feast
    The difference is that you're not here

The many birds we watched still sing
There's pleasure in remembering
    The difference is that you're not here

I see the sky; I hear the song
I still don't know where I belong
    The difference is that you are gone

Beautiful Mountain at Montebello

Who can explain This Mountain's lure
her forest dense, her streams so pure?
The air feels very different here;
it smells so fresh; its sky so clear.

In Autumn, when first lights appear
and brilliant colors chase the drear,
come notes of waking birds in flight,
responding to the changing light.

Forest flowers jut from rocks,
while showing off their striking stalks,
in contrast to those gone before
that now decay on forest floor.

Embracing trees are crimson vines
that climb the trunks of oaks and pines.
Within the glade is open space
that welcomes all to hallowed place.

Sometimes while still in early morn,
and day is not yet fully born,
bright crystal drops adorn fern fronds
and ghostly mists arise from ponds.

In afternoon, shape shifting clouds
reluctantly give up their shrouds,
surrender to the fading light,
enfold The Mountain, signal night.
Night settles in, Darkness descends,
the warmth of daytime sunlight ends.
Nocturnal creatures begin to stir,
some with feathers, some with fur.

They sense Night's music as an inner tune
Nature's call, with which they must commune.
From burrows deep to the mightiest oak,
she protects them well with Darkness' cloak.

We blissfully sleep, quite unaware
of nightly activity taking place there.
The Mountain knows what happens at night
till another day brings benediction in light.

And so it is on the Mountain Beautiful,
Mother Nature remains ever dutiful.
No sooner will glorious Autumn die
than Winter's snowflakes begin to fly

with whispers of future, present and past,
unchanging rhythms, memories that last.
The cycles of seasons all come and go
on the Beautiful Mountain at Montebello.

Chinese Puzzle

Ancient Chinese couple,
pale figures in my garden,
inscrutable, with eyes cast down,

I envy your repose,
your countenance serene,
as from an ancient dynasty,

still listening to a venerable sage,
in harmony with the unseen.

Do words of wisdom echo
from a bygone age?
Discourse as whispers on the winds of mystery?

Perhaps you are at peace;

perhaps you know "The Truth."

Is it
　held in lotus petals?
　still moving on turtle's back?

Or, perhaps,
　soaring on wings of
　dragonflies?

Wild Geese

At twilight a pair made their way across the sky
with no written map or flight plan to tell them where to fly.

Instead, an inner knowing
of the way that they should go.

I thought "how brave,
how fearless,
however can they know
their point of destination or how
to find their flock?"

This passage of the eons is timed
by some inner clock.

If we could understand them,
the stories they would tell.

I envy them.
I wish to trust the universe so well.

The Question

You take me high above the waves,
beyond the far expanses of my consciousness.

Your passion gives me power
like the surf crashing.

When you're not near me there's a void, a silence.

No!....a chasm....unfulfilled.
Where is your voice?

What say the sky....the ocean swell?
They have no message lest you share it.

What is this joy but fleeting thoughts of you that nestle in
and touch my heart

for just an hour, or even just a moment? To see anew the sea
foam, earth, wind, sky –

all blend together with the waves, yet their power cannot
equal ours.

WE meld, WE melt, WE soar above the gulls and wonder….

Can feelings such as this be accidental, caught on the
Karmic pulses of the Universe?

Or worse….

Could this be LOVE?

Forgiveness and Grace

As I remember yesterdays
and think about regrets,
great sadness overcomes me
for sins I can't forget.

Though they were of omission
and had no ill intent
I hear the very road to hell is paved
by deeds that were well meant.

At times I've begged forgiveness of
those who have gone before
I hope that somehow they can know
I understand much more.

My past is part of history
which cannot be undone.
Still, I hope that I'll be absolved
by each and every one

of those I loved but might have hurt
by simple thoughtlessness.
I must believe my sorrow's felt
and they'll see fit to bless.

To reconcile remains of love
from a different time and space,
that love lives on, forgiveness flows
in never ending grace.

The Poetry of Linda Kennedy Partee
Windmills

With poetry inspired by everyday surroundings: nature, books, art, music and life events, Linda's mind spins with ideas for creating poems using a variety of formats and techniques. By thoughtfully matching form-to-subject, both the power and emotion of her work is enhanced for the reader. Selections of her poetry have been published and recognized with awards. A native Californian and career educator, Linda resides in Williamsburg, and is a member of the Poetry Society of Virginia, The James City Poets, Cercle de Plume, and the Creative Writer's Critique. As a poet, she is also a workshop instructor.

Lost Abundance

Inspiration: *A Message from Martha* by Mark Avery

Oh, Martha, could you mourn what you'd not known?
Can we long for something we've never seen?
A caged-captive all your twenty-nine years,
did DNA codes tug at your wild roots?

More than a century now since your demise
as the last Passenger Pigeon on earth.
"First Lady" of your species to the end--
death professed you "Last Lady" of your kind.

Like parallel rivers, colonists poured
across the land spoiling most in their path,
while your colonies flooded skies to black.
Trees still live who were shaken by your wind.

As food and nesting resources grew scant
in the name of progress, starvation ruled.
You, the most common bird on our planet,
of a species once numbering billions.

Were you aware you were gregarious--
a wandering nomad by nature?
Did you think about lurking predators…
..the wolf, fox, eagle, squirrel or shotgun?

You never dived from clouds to make deer run,
or applaud your wings to announce scarce food.
Did you feel the urge, the pull of seasons,
or live by not really living at all?

Yours, a visible and rare extinction
going quickly from familiar to not,
for as man won the West, he lost the Wild
when progress upset life's subtle balance.

~POSTSCRIPT~

Resurrected in Smithsonian glass,
you grasp the last branch of your family tree,
ever-watchful of events that left you,
alone, to shoulder your species history.

Eden's Garden

Duck your head beneath the arbor,
sit your bones upon the bench;
gaze about you at the roses,
meet the poet in their midst.

Pierre De Ronsard is the namesake,
though we call her Eden Rose;
true romantic and great beauty,
Ooo-la-la French femme fatale.

You'll be smitten by her presence,
tendrils climbing everywhere;
faintly fragrant, faintly blushing,
double cream poured in a cup.

Huge and heavy are her blossoms,
lush and full describe her life;
sister-kin dance all around her,
showing off the blooming bride.

Eden stole my heart and garden,
and will charm and steal your's too.
What once was mine can no more be,
for it all belongs to her.

Sea Life

~ *A Sonnet* ~

We scatter loved ones ashes on the sea,
returning them to arms of ancient waves;
no longer bound to earth, we set them free--
transmuting their remains beyond mere graves.

A scrub of salt will strip away the past,
imagined sins absolved, completely cleansed
by ocean's grand confessor holding fast;
departed souls made ready to transcend.

Perhaps soul-seeds return to land, spit out
by giant mammal jaws like Jonah's whale.
Suppose recycled souls behold no doubt
about rebirth, while waiting air's inhale.

So should you feel you've been at sea before,
it could be that you've stepped once more ashore.

Women of a Certain Age

Lady-like, she sits in the waiting room of extinction,
her eyes sharp and twinkling with intelligence,
making peace with the truth that placed her here.
Aware that many past learnings had become obsolete,
and her own teenage years more unique than most--
this remnant of the '50s sighs deeply.

Once, perched on the cusp of time that poured the
foundation for adulthood,
she and her peers had been raised to be obedient,
respectful, modest and mannerly--inheriting
their parents puritan work ethic and views of the world,
seldom deviating from the route laid out for them.

The cultural revolution of the '60s
created chaos in the roots of many budding adults.
She and her ilk confused as to who and how to please,
since few felt the freedom to please themselves,
so they turned a critical eye on those who succumbed
to rock 'n roll, sex and drugs.
A developmental gap opened wide--one never filled.

Carrying forward the traditions instilled in their past,
these reliable young housewives and mothers
turned a deaf ear to the lure of wild music,
a raised eyebrow to the immodesty of sex,
and tsk-tsk'd against dope, while smoking Virginia Slims.

Unable to bend in the wind of extraordinary change,
without time to bend, they lost a decade of American life
that would influence times to come.

New movements gained strength and popularity
leaving these women overwhelmed and guilt-ridden.
Family life changed forever, nudging
these sweet young things onto a fast-track
that left them wondering what had happened
to their plans and dreams.

At home they became CEO of everything "household",
work horses in their careers, and
decked-out arm-candy in their free time,
which really wasn't free.
Divorce and breakdowns became the slap of reality.

Increasingly invisible and ignored by entitled youth,
for ladies of a certain age, time slipped through fingers.
There would be no going back…no do-overs.
Society tossed them social media devices to stay in touch,
pretending that FaceBook could replace human touch.
Now, one ill-equipped pretender sits, waiting her turn
to be phased-out, an aberration of nature's throes of change,
who still remembers that the fork goes on the left,
knife and spoon on the right.

Tangled Roots

~A Ballad of the Blue Ridge Mountains~

Old Blue Ridge sounds still haunt the air
with songbird's hungry pip;
where rivers bubble, rush and fall
while winds caress or whip.

The native tribes made music there
on ancient hunting grounds,
then English, Irish, Scot and Welsh
united all these sounds.

They moved diverse ideas forth
with homeland tools and croons,
expanding music's poetry
with old-time fiddlin' tunes.

The blacks brought banjo's stringy roots
to shape this cultural stew--
the core of string-band instruments
and lonesome vocal blues.

Hard-scrabble lives in folksong birthed
a pluckin', strummin' style;
with country gospels riffed in verse
to gather up a smile.

New bluegrass songs will haunt the air
together with the old,
and lift the souls of mountain ghosts--
their Blue Ridge stories told.

The Family Tree

Generations tumble forward like a waterfall,
umbilical clouds betrothed to earth
bequeathing a measured flow of celestial breath.
Begetting is but one raindrop
beholding another and uniting
to form a trickle, a stream, a river--
tributaries flowing, branching, merging,
rushing……always rushing.

Pushing blindly through insistent currents,
drifting, mingling, swirling, eroding,
Begottens must plunge over the precipice
into a bottomless abyss--
an out-of-sight unknown, waiting
to gather them, cradle and embrace them;
to soothe them from another
tumultuous ancestral journey.

Ashes to ashes, dust to dust,
raindrop to raindrop,
they rise in misty vapor
to descend again.

Salem Soliloquy
(Massachusetts, 1692)

Devils wearin' church face, church face, church face
Devils with their church mask on.
Devils wearin' church face, church face, church face
Devils with their church mask on.

Hee-hee, hi-hi, ho-ho, hum
Look out Salem, here they come--
Wearin' pious faces, sayin' prayers on end,
Holdin' far-fetched suspicion of a neighbor or a friend.
Accusers are the young girls barkin' like the dog,
Spewin' curses from their lips, croakin' like a frog.

Devils wearin' church face, church face, church face
Devils with their church mask on.

First, have the Doctor examine and conclude,
"Gotta handful of witchcraft startin' up a feud".
Behavin' so peculiar, instillin' fear in most,
Showin' all the townfolk Satan is their host.
Pointin' skinny fingers, doomin' elders straight to hell,
Blamin' them for the curse of their black magic spell.

Devils wearin' church face, church face, church face
Devils with their church mask on.

Superstitious gossip is the wick that fuels your mess,
As more and more innocents are forced to confess
Startin' in the morning into winter's early night,
Gallows hang the guiltless because of your own fright.
God forgive you Salem, better drop to your knees
And beg His pardon for these necks that you squeeze.

Devils wearin' church face, church face, church face
Devils with their church mask on.

Hee-hee, hi-hi, ho-ho, hum
Look out Salem, here they come--
Powerless young maidens still cravin' bright light
Will spread their lies all dressed in white.
Tight-collared clergy and frock-coated jury
Damn those accused in quite a big hurry.
In spite of the evidence, defined by men,
Twenty unjust murders did happen then.
Amen, brother, amen.

Devils wearin' church face, church face, church face,
Devils with their church mask on.
Devils wearin' church face, church face, church face,
Devils with their church mask on.

Pomp & Circumstances

The air undulates with heat and the long day begins
as it always does, on this day of expectations.
Come together for its unfolding and sing its spirited songs.
Listen to snapping breeze-caught cloth and remember why.

Make ready to feel the steady drumming thunder,
to hear the fluting gathering calls of pipes;
their cadence marking the coming of corps and banners,
marching in waves of brotherly configurations.

Picnics spread, feeding visions of our forefathers,
drunk from sipping at the well of courage.
Drowsy babes and restless children on blanketed grass wait;
window-framed faces and chairs on cracked porches,
anticipate.

Furtive eyes search the sky for a dusky curtain to descend,
while arms link and hands clasp, on this eve of celebration.
Reunion, symbol of old war reflections, sighs of promise,
as chins lift toward the darkening of the night.

Like cannon's shot, the birth of freedom repeats its cry,
unleashed in a fiery brilliance of dreams.
Reminders of a long-ago pledge, each spark a patriot
living on through a cacophony by design.

Air is stilled with ash-fall when the long day finally yawns,
as it always does, following this ritual of renewal.
Once complacent hearts carry freedom's beat,
drafting the vows of future guardians to its cause.

The Taste Of Conversation

Recall the flavored words of young romance,
those waltz-time murmurings of sweet nothings,
like pink-boxed creampuffs delicately soft
with sugared sentiments and lip-licked dreams.

Forever friendships speak of yesterdays--
"remember whens" and "have you heard abouts"--
hors d'oeuvres before tomorrow's plat du jour;
aged cheese and wine that linger long on tongues.

In pressure cooker times for raising kids,
can parents manage meaningful exchange
between the Lucky Charms and fast food foil?
Is wisdom's flavor slurped or dumped as trash?

Do hand-held gadgets fill the emptiness--
those forkless, habit-forming finger foods?
Addictive like a bag of salty chips,
they don't ease hunger more than biting nails.

A Capitol Affair

Performing briefly every spring, we watch
unfurling costumes shaken loose and plumped,
appearing silently all powdered-pink
until they fill the stage with quiet grace
to dip and sway to secret melodies,
like Geisha's trained for entertainment's joys.

Endearments sweetly whispered fill the air
like butterfly flirtations, velvet-veiled
to kiss their minions cheeks with innocence--
a barely-there confetti silk caress.
Embraced and smitten, wrapped in beauty's spell,
admirers play their part in nature's scene.

Without an audience, would dancers bow
or twirl and rustle clustered coronets;
would tiptoed prancers scatter carefree charms,
and ballerinas toss kimonos free?
One blink, quick wink before the magic fades,
when cherry blossoms crown a nation's throne.

Dancing The Seasons

~lyrics to the tune of "Morning Has Broken"~

Springtime unfolding, earth has awakened
Heartstrings are playing, tunes for the dance;
Promise and dreamtime, mem'ries are born here
Waltzing life's raindrops spins the romance.

Embrace the summer, grow with the season,
Tend to life's garden, fruits of your hand;
Visions will flourish, grab the ring swiftly,
Living each moment of hourglass sand.

Open your mind's eye, count every blessing
Blazing with color, autumn's ballet;
Harvest and gather what you have planted,
Sprinkled with teardrops, your life's bouquet.

Over your shoulder, winter is coming
Beauty in pearl-grey, windblown like leaves.
Unlace your burdens, find peace and fly free
Wonder the myst'ry your story weaves.

Dancing Moonlight Garden

Blank Verse

Romantic dreams inspired her flowerbeds
around the pond and up a fence to cling.
Behind the house, a patch of space remained
for dancing moonlight's garden; bridal whites
with candle glow reflecting ghostly blooms
like clematis, gardenia, jasmine, rose,
midst fragrant hint of honeysuckle vine.

She sowed her chosen flora, waiting growth
to match the sweeping fullness that her gown
produced when gliding over stones at dark.
Rehearsing visions, no partner in sight,
she wiled away the evening hours of youth
perfecting nature's stage with empty arms
because no mate exactly fit her scheme.

With hair gone white, mature like buds unfurled,
she sits and gazes down from window's perch;
old music playing, drifts like memories--
wallflower's moonlit waltz among her kind,
she yearns for shoes that meet hers toe-to-toe.
Imagination leaves her breathless still;
her heart holds hope for moonlight garden's dance.

Heartsong

~A Ballad~

In dark despair she lay her head
on pillows made of silk;
her arms as empty as her heart,
still urging mother's milk.

Poor babe, he did not live one day,
long sought, then quickly gone;
now heaven holds her child, her dream,
since cold and misty dawn.

> *"Be sweet, be tender," spills her song,*
> *"and love him like I could;*
> *my name please whisper near his cheek*
> *in comfort, as I would."*

> *"Stay close about so he'll not fear*
> *or ever feel alone;*
> *then teach him patience for my face,*
> *the first face he was shown."*

One day her spirit will fly free,
unbound by earthly things;
her babe and she will meet again
to tie loose apron strings.

A Reckoning

Inspiration: A Year by the Sea (Joan Anderson)

1. Summer

On damp and dazzled sand-duned beach
she digs up wayward heart and soul
where tidal waves of anguish form.
There drifts a song sung by the sea,
from salt-filled crest, crescendos rise
to find her wounds and lick the pain
like old tattoos remember ink.

Selecting freedom's time and space,
no one to please except herself,
dissecting promises and dreams,
thoughts ride in whispers on sea's breeze.
The water laps and pools her angst,
then gently under foot dissolves
'til still and stagnant just as she.

2. Autumn

Devotion given, self adrift
from those she loves and leaves behind,
untethered, not unsevered heart,
held breath released upon the waves.
Performance crisis, role unclear,
ambivalence her island fort;
she strands herself alone to grieve.

Bravado wanes, the senses yield
all pricked and sharp like broken shells.
She tunes to nature's beckoning
where truth intrudes her doubt-filled mind
and begs her listen…feel…observe;
to end charades, unknot regrets
and reach beyond this shadowed life.

3. Winter

As pewter fog slips in like eels,
illusion wakes confusion's sleep,
delusion's oft-forgotten truth:
alone and lonely aren't the same.
Upheaval's turmoil gnaws earth's crust
and gathers passions deep inside
without constraint, obliging none.

Wet soulful eyes now recognize
those second-fiddle days gone by--
the tune that played from then 'til now
has finished. Overtures await.
She hesitates with cautious strokes
to swim or drown, the choice is hers,
no lifeguard bars one's strength of will.

4. Spring

A seaside spell like magic strikes,
and makes a childlike, carefree splash,
to take a risk in naked bliss
amid suspended space and time.
Migration over-head, beneath,
within--which signals moving on
to leave fresh footprints leading home.

Earth's dome of sky and bowl of sea,
where edges blur and corners hide,
protects the souls who've lost their way.
So insecure and barely there,
they trust the sea to wash their dreams
to higher ground which can be found
untrod--a soothing, smoothing place.

Saint Augustine In His Cell

(Botticelli @ 1494)

The canvas small and easily ignored
is the one which catches my attentive eye,
but not because of brushstrokes, colors, style--
it's what's been freely tossed upon the floor
around a fervent writer's saintly feet.

Spent quills are there with crumpled paper wads--
collapsed attempts at ideas and thoughts
which symbolize creation's birthing pains--
delivering the **new** to open hands
once words and purpose are clearly aligned.

A haloed saint at work in semi-dark,
although it could be you or even me
rejecting thoughts and dropping them aside.
Composing's act and art quite similar
among us--sleuths uncaging perfect words,
releasing heartfelt truth to ink and script.

The Poetry of Mark Reardon
Roots and Wings

Mark A. Reardon was born and raised in the beautiful Adirondack Mountains of New York. He served in the U.S. Army for forty-four years as soldier and civilian.

Mark began his writing career in a beginning poetry-writing workshop with the Christopher Wren Association at The College of William and Mary, and has continued to develop his skills in local workshops. He is the author of the historical novel, Sarah, A Forgotten Patriot. He also published poetry in an anthology entitled: Distant Horizons, as Seen By Williamsburg Poets.

He lives in Williamsburg with his wife Cindi

Roots and Wings

Today as we watched you try your new wings
We knew you must leave to make your own way.
We know not what perils the world will bring.
If we could, we would always have you stay.

But it is God's law, youth must ever fly.
As you leave we wonder what you'll recall.
Will you think of us as you glide on high?
We pray your roots will keep you from a fall.

Roots are a piece of the soul that nourish
Dreams and values that tie us to our past.
May yours be strong and grant your every wish.
And may your heart remember to the last,

We gave you roots so you'd have strength and love.
We gave you wings so you could soar above.

First Love

When did we first fall in love?
Was it that day when we first kissed?
That first clinch sure made me quiver.
Was that the day we fell in love?

Was it the day when we first kissed?
All I remember of that day is the thrill
of holding your body close
and your lips touching mine.

That first clinch sure made me quiver.
The clinch has turned to an embrace.
Today we melt together as one
and your touch is all I know of love.

Was that the day we fell in love?
I don't know.
All I know is your kiss still thrills me
and when we embrace I still quiver.

Spring Cleaning

Once a year, as ordained by God, a miracle occurs.
The air turns warm and cheerful,
And the verdant greens of spring
Replace the dreary grays of winter.

As the Good Lord changes the world's scenery
A woman wakes from her winter's slumber and announces:
"Today we will begin spring cleaning.
And I expect everyone to help."

Children shriek in fear and rush to get to school
(Even if it is not in session).
The ninety pound dog cowers
And looks for cover that cannot be found.

Yes the "Mrs. Hyde of the Vacuum" has been unleashed
With powers that would make a super hero envy.
And I am left alone to defend myself from
This creature who on other days would be my wife.

Every piece of furniture will be moved and moved again.
No speck of dirt or dust will miss her attention. Heavy
Machinery that could suck the chrome off a Harley Davidson
roars to life, the music of this crazed annual ritual.

The rumble of vacuum and shampooer
Fill the air from dawn to darkened night.
Unintelligible growls emerge from her body
As she recovers things long thought lost forever.

At last the house is returned to order.
As she sits upon her throne admiring all she surveys
I breathe a sigh of relief as she utters this final refrain:
"I'll break the legs of anyone I catch eating in this living room."

Children and dog cautiously return
Knowing they are safe, at least until fall.

I Fell In Love With You Anew

I fell in love with you anew this morn.
As I watched you sleep in the early light,
I saw the girl for whom my love was born
and once again my youthful heart took flight.
I fell in love with you anew today.
As I watched the woman who fills my life
I saw your beauty as a sweet bouquet
and I thanked God you deigned to be my wife.
I fell in love with you anew this eve.
As I watched you rest in the afterglow
I saw the artful magic you still weave,
that stole my heart so very long ago.
My life with you has been a dream come true.
Each day with you I fall in love anew

Lucinda

When I am old and grey
And sitting by the fire,
I'll close my eyes and pray.
I'll thank God you chose me
      To share your desire.

I'll dream of the beauty of your youth
And the gentleness of your touch.
I'll whisper once again those words of truth,
"I will never love anyone as much."

As the fire and a blanket warm my body,
Thoughts of you will warm my heart.
Once again I'll languish in your spirit free
And know we shall never grow apart.

Though time may bring some other women a furrow,
Your face will ever be as soft and young
As it was when first I saw your eyes aglow
And in each other's arms we clung.

Then, even as the fire starts to fade
My face will smile in the night's shade.
Because you brought love into my life
By agreeing to be my wife.

Mom

I never really knew her,
But I will always cherish her memory.

I did not know her when she was small
Or know of what dreams she dreamt.
I did not know her when she was young
And full of life and gaiety.

I did not know her when she met her life's love,
Or what she was thinking the day she became a bride.
I did not know her when her first born came,
Or even when four more arrived.

I did not know her when she scrimped
To feed a family fighting through a depression.
Nor did I know her when she planted
A victory garden to help win a war.

I never knew what thoughts
Went through her mind.
And I never knew what dreams
She left behind.

I never really knew her,
But I will always cherish her memory.

I knew her in her middle years,
A wife, a homemaker, a mother of seven.
There was nothing she could not do
And she always had time for everyone.

I remember her there each morning when I awoke,
And when I came home from school.
I remember her days spent cooking for us
And sewing for others to bring in a few extra dollars.

I remember her in the evening
Sitting in her rocker knitting presents for Christmas.
I remember her stopping whatever she was doing
To sit and talk to with friends who always came by.

I remember her sitting at her table
Telling stories of her life long ago,
And doling out her wisdom
With a gentle nudge to always do right.

I remember her in her later years
Crying for the only man she ever loved,
And for the sons she had outlived
Yet accepting her fate with grace and strength.

No, I guess I never really knew my mother,
But I will always cherish her memory.

Sunday Morning Services

Sunday Breakfast was a moveable feast,
The one meal my father cooked every week.
From dawn on the house was filled with rich aromas,
Coffee, eggs, bacon and sausage, enough to feed the neighbors.
Mother held court ensconced in her throne,
A simple chair at the head of her table.
From there she dispensed history, wisdom, condolences and joy.
People of every ilk from throughout the village
Stopped in for an audience, coffee, nosh, and conversation.
No appointment was needed
But each seemed to have an appointed time
And each had an appointed seat at her table.
No topic of the day was left undiscussed,
And somehow each person knew their time was up
As a new visitor arrived to take their place.
I could only stand, listen and marvel
Never wanting it to end.
But at noon all audiences came to an end.
Sunday Dinner was another ritual that needed her attention.

Neil

He was a leprechaun of a man,
Irish through and through.
Five feet five he stood,
Yet no man stood taller than he.

His smile disarmed you
As his blue eyes consumed you.
You could not help but like him
As his silver tongue beguiled you.

When he entered a bar, as he often did,
Men stood aside to make room for him.
He chased his shots with swallows of beer
As he held court with anyone near.

He worked three jobs to feed his brood.
He was proud that his house he owned.
He would not allow his family to need.
And charity was to be given not received.

He cried when "Danny Boy" was sung
And laughed out loud at Bob Hope's jokes.
He loved his wife and hugged her tight
And always kissed her good night.

He was on a first name basis with the Monsignor.
And though his attendance at Mass could be improved
Sure it was to him his God was real
And daily they conversed without the need to kneel.

When on St Patty's Eve his days were done
He went with a smile.
Perhaps, it was the sight of new mown Irish sod,
Or maybe, he was just sharing a joke with God.

He lived his life to its fullest
And gave joy to all who knew him.
His is a legacy I'm proud to share,
He was indeed a leprechaun of a man.

The Power of Children To Change One's Life

With what were we thinking
when we decided to procreate?
It all happened in a blinking;
now we live on bicarbonate.

When small they had us up at all hours.
Their every wish was our command.
Where did they get those mighty powers?
I confess I do not understand.

Before we knew it they were teens.
Why did God create teenage boys and girls?
The Good Lord can be very mean.
He did not even warn us of the perils.

But there's a power greater than us all.
As I watch my children try to navigate
the snares they created conjugal,
I smile and offer them the bicarbonate.

Dad

He never tried to be my best friend.
He never played ball with me
Nor did he ever come to my games.
He never had sage advice
Nor was he the one I went to for comfort.
So why did I always like the man?

He loved one woman until the day he died.
He helped raise seven "only children."
He always worked three jobs
To give us what we needed
And sometimes what we wanted.
He never imposed his will upon me
To try to make me something I was not.
He had but one rule to live by,
"Do not make your mother mad."
The violation of which could bring
Punishment swift and harsh.
He didn't always agree with decisions that I made.
But was always there to back me up.
When I got myself in over my head
And thought that I might fail,
I could always turn and see him there.
His silence told me all would be okay.
He shined my shoes for church.
He taught me to keep score for a baseball game
On a Saturday afternoon before he went to work.

He woke up early to get my papers ready,
Before going off to work.
And after a hard day at the factory,
He helped me with my spelling, math and catechism.

He never asked for thanks and always seemed grateful
For the little I gave him in return.
He taught me of pride and respect and honor.
And he taught me what it meant to be a father.
For the all things he did, I guess I not only liked the man,
I loved him more than these feeble words can tell.

Pet Peeve

Now my wife says I may be too fussy.
But there's one thing that really annoys me,
It's the chaos that occurs whenever
My children are placed in the role of planner.

Yes, I may be a bit picayune.
But when I'm told something is to happen at noon,
I have (I am told) an unreasonable expectation
that it will occur sometime within my anticipation.

But time has no meaning to these children of mine.
To them seven might just as well be quarter past nine.
For a man who believes that ten minutes early is late,
These procrastinators profoundly aggravate.

But timing is only the beginning of their torture of me.
For when they finally arrive I'm forced to question their ancestry.
They have no idea what they are about
Let alone a plan to ease my doubt.

To think that my days may one day be placed in their hands,
And that I could be put under their commands,
Gives me reason to pause and wonder with gravity,
Will they be on time to bury me?

Kindness

Kindness is:
Kissing when we're sad; it's the
Karat we measure love by; it generates
Kaleidoscopes of color in our hearts and minds; it's
Knowing there is good in the world; it
Kindles warmth and joy. It is the
Keystone of life.

Kindness is:
Keeping promises to all; it's being the
Keeper of secrets big and small; it's the
Knowledge that we are loved; it's loving
Kith, kin and all mankind; it's doing
Kind acts for no reason. It is the
Keystone of life.

Show Me

As we go out on our weekly adventures,
I know the things we look at are the same.
But what are you seeing?

What are you thinking as you pick that dandelion
 for your Mommy?
As we traverse the deep dark forest
 Full of "elefunks" and "woosels,"
What goes through your mind?
What are you seeing as the squirrels scurry away from us?
What feelings make you giggle
While the cool water laps at our bare feet
As we walk along the beach?
And as you look out into that ocean of a lake,
 What do you see?
How big is your world?
Is everything you see perfect?

Won't you please show me the world,
As only you and God truly see it?

A Child's Love Will Overcome All

The smoke from the burning towers
Choked the nation and brought tears to our eyes.
Born in terror and irrational hatred,
What callous minds could conceive such horror?

Her innocent beauty like a fresh ocean breeze,
Blew the smoke and tears from our eyes.
Born in the shadow of this smoke and carnage
Her birth brought love and joy back into our lives.

While the world watched the towers fall,
The cowards claimed they did it for God.
They rejoice in death, darkness and misery.
But no God will ever forgive their perfidy.

Instead, He smiles on this new born babe
And we rejoice in her life and the light it brings,
For the love one innocent child brings into the world
Will always defeat hatred and perversity.

Lucinda Jean Reardon born 16 September 2001

Cody

Lie there in the sun and rest old dog,
You've earned that quiet spot.
This family owes you for all you gave
And it will not be forgot.

You entertained us when you were young.
You herded cats and kept them at bay.
You never failed to make us laugh
As you chased and jumped and played.

Your brown eyes shined like gentle rays of love.
You always knew when we needed petting.
You protected us as by our beds you laid,
And our secrets you always kept without fretting.

Your step slowed, or maybe it was ours.
Maybe you slowed down to help us on our walks,
Or simply to extend them a little while longer.
Or maybe - just to remind us to enjoy our little talks.

You taught us how to love without question.
So now rest easy old friend.
We'll always love you and hold you dear.
And to all your needs, God will attend.

And on some future sunny day
I know that we shall meet again.
And we shall all be young once more
And you will bring our joy back then.

The Poetry of Terry Shephard
The Way We Love

Terry Shepard has been a resident of Williamsburg since 1984. She was born in Verdun, France to a military father stationed there. She grew up in Newport News and attended Virginia Commonwealth University where she earned a baccalaureate degree in commercial art. After graduation Terry worked for NASA, Langley Research Center, first as a technical and scientific photographer, then a director, writer, and producer of documentaries. She currently enjoys writing poetry with the James City Poets, illustrating, spending time with her grandson, and gardening.

Life's Moment

She called to him from the pear tree,
an exited pulsating twitter.
He came to her,
                in his cardinal coat,
landed, fluffed his feathers.
They hopped to lower branches,
then into the hedge
                where home was.
She hesitated on the edge
waiting for him to admire,
                her first egg.
Then, she settled in,
pushed her body fully round her bundle.
He watched,
                silently perched.
I saw in him my husband's eyes
when we were young,
and a bump in my belly
                stilled the moments,
and I felt the essence of all those paintings
of Mary and Joseph and
                a miracle in a manger.

I Dreamed

I dreamed a son
so many years before I meet him.
Blue eyes, warm smile, brown hair,
I dreamed how it felt to hold him.
I dreamed a son.

I dreamed a little boy
so many years before he was one.
Skinned knees, brave heart, big smile,
I dreamed what it felt to know him.
I dreamed a little boy.

I dreamed motherhood
so many years before I was one.
Warm home, much love, kind words,
I dreamed a family.
I dreamed until I had one.

I nurtured a little boy
on his way to manhood.
Teen years, heart ache, long roads,
I nurtured a little boy
until he was grown and had one.

I never dreamed my current roll.
Grandma I am called,
warm soul, so thankful, in awe
I never dreamed the little boy
who captures my heart now.

I Write

I write without pencil or pen,
when taking a walk, I let my thoughts in.
I write through all of the day,
changing pictures to words, to fashion the play.
I write before falling asleep
in those moments when all my thoughts seep
onto a night journey's stage
then I wake and put pencil to page.

I write because of the ease
of remembering sunny splashed seas.
I write to let beauty in,
to remember the moments of Zen.
I write because I'm on earth,
where smelly swamp bogs give birth.
I write to watch memories swim
as if I could live them again.

Struck by Cupid's Arrow

He's really cupid:
introduces Lolita to the new goat Joe,
opens the pen to let her next mate in,
tells Bessie she'll have a calf come summer,
pats her weighted growing sides,
checks on the chicks in the incubator,
takes Bull rabbit to the field
where a harem eats wild clover,
fixes the fence, pulls the barbed wire,
plows the meadow. I know he knows
when he drew his bow:
shoot his arrow at me,
changed my dreams,
looked with coy eyes,
listened intently.
I know he knows, why he drew his bow.

What We Leave Behind

The mothers
of the old neighborhood
are like actors in a play now,
somewhere in my mind,
history I remember,
while strolling the old stage.

Their story
is like "Murder She Wrote",
only no one was ever murdered.
They were taken by natural causes.
And I think. How can it be natural,
to lose a whole generation to time?

Should I call out their names:
Mrs. Lake and Mrs. Schroeder,
Mrs. Edwards, Mrs. Evitts,
Mrs. Gunn and Mrs. Mulleins?
Should I speak their titles:
Judy Milne's mom,
Herby Hendrickson's mother?

The snow and slush of today
soups toward gutters,
flower tips peek out from old beds,
a few buds hug old branches.
And I think. I'm older now than the
mother's I remember.
When did they become characters
my daughter-in-laws age?

They are snap shots:
youthful and splendid,
speaking their children's names,
in German and Vietnamese,
with accents from Texas,
California, New York.
They are cooking and kneeling,
mowing lawns, hauling groceries,
smiling, talking in yards
and at dining room tables,
inhabiting houses I knew -
where light beams flow through windows,
across floors, through door ways,
halting shadows that never grew.

They are saying with every gesture
with every word I can remember,
that motherhood has meaning,
life is worth living,
love grows the next generation.

> They left behind
> the way they loved.
> The way we love is
> all we leave behind.

Vibrations of Voice

Dialed numbers transmit
across valleys and deltas,
time zones and deserts,
and two mountain ranges,
through high winds and soft winds
and northern clippers,
bouncing past towers
and satellite dishes,
until they reach intended receiver.

Receiver reacts
becomes a transmitter,
across byways and highways
and rising deep rivers,
across continental divide
and thick dark forest,
through dampness and dryness
and cloud covered steeples.

Vibrations of voice
transformed through waves,
blending her lunch time
and my dinner time ways.
Grandchildren in back ground,
we talk and we laugh.
Receiver, transmitter
enjoy a chat about
science and medical health,
marvels of nature
and new baby's birth.

"Isn't it something.
I had one boy and one girl,
now each of my children have
one boy and one girl,
and my granddaughter
just had a daughter, now she has
one boy and one girl.
What are the statistics of that
in this world?"

"Remember how your father
called your mother mate.
Was he reminding her, he was her equal?"
We laugh and retell the story
of their war time romance -
ship yard welder mates,
working side by side
not knowing the other
until her mother took her shield off,
and he realized
his mate was a girl.
He fell in love right then.
"Do you think they ever imagined
two grandchildren,
four great grandchildren,
two great, great grandchildren?"

"If they could see the world now."
We wish we could give them a call,
across ages and a century of change
and heavenly stars
thru ethos and cosmos
where ever they are.

Butterfly Glide

The first time I saw a butterfly glide
it lifted gently on prevailing wind,
buffeted its edges from side to side
and sailed on magical thermal rise.

I focused my eyes on its yellow wings,
a living kite floating on breeze.
It soared like an eagle thru the sky,
tilted its body, circled round,

landed on poppies ten inches high.
It moved without flutter or flapping arms,
moved with a silence I've never known.
Soared like an eagle in the sky,

landed on poppies ten inches high.

In His Wallet

In his wallet
there's a picture of a boy
who will some day grow
into the large teeth in his mouth
and the tee shirt that droops,
but will never live long enough
to have children.
There are no other pictures
tucked into folds
placed in places his mind
could wander.
One picture says everything
that matters.
The confident ten year old
chose him to have the picture,
wrote I love you on the back,
with squiggly script.

In his wallet
there is carefully considered
squiggly script that
keeps this man a father.

Ode to My Lost Uterus

Heart of my heart
you found the place of peace
when my brain was injured.
You grew the space
like a plant growing root and leaf
that connected me
between earth and sky.
Deep inside my abdomen
you rose the tides,
cradled the fetus
created life.

How could you get confused
grown a mass,
then drop
upon my bladder,
like a alien in grief?
Removed by surgeon's blade,
heart of my heart,
you should have grown old
with the rest of me,
partnered in friendship
the changes of age,
been the wise old crone
with the looking glass.

Secret Love

I awoke to clash in thunder skies,
and burst of rain that opened my sleepy eyes.
I missed the twilight sounds of feathered beings
that rested from their usual sunrise singing.

On broken stems, the last iris blooms
lie thinly draped upon the soggy loam,
their fragile color melts into the ground,
while carnations turn a soppy hue of brown.

Like the rabbit nestled in its burrow
napping thru the rolling distant rumble,
I waited out the early morning rain
to find new growth with a weather change.

Shoots of red calla lilies rise,
where once yellow daffodils had died.
Pushed thru the mulch, tiny cleome climb
where little blue forget-me-nots look fine.

I putter in the freshly moistened dirt
my heart filled with my secret love, "the earth,"
where air is free to breath, and nurture life,
through sudden storms and distant looming strife.

The "Art of Aging"

"If I Were a Vintage Sports Car"

If I were a vintage sports car I'd blame my low energy on lack of petrol. Which I'd gladly receive and soon be knocking down the highway. My sputtered start I'd blame on carbon build up, 'til moaning cough turned to purr and wheels triumph the pavement. Missing parts I'd just ignore. Accept my newer replacements without a care. They'd fit well lubed, bolted, and snapped, while synthetic oil floated my pistons. I'd shine from being buffed and not a dent or scuff would blunder my reflection. Attracted to other carbon beginnings my hood would rumble when I see one admiring my condition. Why I'd hold back a laugh when some young being knowing the history of my vintage would lean over me, rub me smoothly, and leave a gasp of his hot breath upon my surface. He'd wipe it off with the cuff of his sleeve pulled over the palm of his hand. If I were lucky I'd leave with him, one who would be admiring and lovely, keeping me restored until he started his own family. Then I'd be passed on as if being reincarnated into the life of another young admirer. There'd be nothing wrong with being a sports car. I'd skip those nursing homes with disgruntled attendants. I doubt I'd ever sit out in a yard, up on blocks with rusted spots, showing my age in disgraceful dissatisfying renditions.

Flight

Atmospheric shift shows
on barometric gauge,
pressure in her feathers twitch
to end of summer days.

Forecast is for wind.
complete with sweeping cold,
science calculates,
her wings predict snow.

She says goodbye to nesting
before the steeping storms
on currents slipping southward
toward a rising dawn.

I also feel the call of fall
in pockets of stalled air,
their bump and grind predicting
winter's coming near.

I'd like to be nomadic
lift my wings and glide
as if some force from long ago
said, "You were meant to fly."

Mortality

Consciousness
sweeps and swirls
on an energy flow:
external, internal,
foreign, familiar,
collects thoughts,
defines, redefines,
glimpses self
as moments in time.

The Letting Go

Sometimes it does not help to know
that everyone goes through this,
the letting go,
and I think, how much that sounds like oh.
Oh, my God the letting go.

I know that healing comes in waves
with peeks that crest in undertows,
the turning back,
the letting go.
Oh, my God the letting go.

CPSIA information can be obtained at www.ICGtesting.com
Printed in the USA
BVIW12n1837191217
503237BV00011B/204